NEW DIRECTIONS FOR YOUTH DEVELOPMENT

Theory
Practice
Research

fall | 2011

Expanded Learning Time and Opportunities

Helen Janc Malone | *issue editor*

Gil G. Noam
Editor-in-Chief

JOSSEY-BASS™
An Imprint of
WILEY

Expanded Learning Time and Opportunities
Helen Janc Malone (ed.)
New Directions for Youth Development, No. 131, Fall 2011
Gil G. Noam, Editor-in-Chief
This is a peer-reviewed journal.

Microfilm copies of issues and articles are available in 16mm and 35mm, as well as microfiche in 105mm, through University Microfilms Inc., 300 North Zeeb Road, Ann Arbor, MI 48106-1346.

New Directions for Youth Development is indexed in Academic Search (EBSCO), Academic Search Premier (EBSCO), Contents Pages in Education (T&F), Current Abstracts (EBSCO), Educational Research Abstracts Online (T&F), EMBASE/Excerpta Medica (Elsevier), ERIC Database (Education Resources Information Center), Index Medicus/MEDLINE/PubMed (NLM), MEDLINE/PubMed (NLM), SocINDEX (EBSCO), Sociology of Education Abstracts (T&F), and Studies on Women & Gender Abstracts (T&F).

NEW DIRECTIONS FOR YOUTH DEVELOPMENT (ISSN 1533-8916, electronic ISSN 1537-5781) is part of the Jossey-Bass Psychology Series and is published quarterly by Wiley Subscription Services, Inc., A Wiley Company, at Jossey-Bass, One Montgomery Street, Suite 1200, San Francisco, CA 94104-4594. POSTMASTER: Send address changes to New Directions for Youth Development, Jossey-Bass, One Montgomery Street, Suite 1200, San Francisco, CA 94104-4594.

SUBSCRIPTIONS for individuals cost $89.00 for U.S./Canada/Mexico; $113.00 international. For institutions, agencies, and libraries, $281.00 U.S.; $321.00 Canada/Mexico; $355.00 international. Prices subject to change. Refer to the order form that appears at the back of most volumes of this journal.

EDITORIAL CORRESPONDENCE should be sent to the Editor-in-Chief, Dr. Gil G. Noam, McLean Hospital, Harvard Medical School, 115 Mill Street, Belmont, MA 02478.

Cover photograph by kirin_photo/©iStockphoto (RF)

www.josseybass.com

Contents

Issue Editor's Notes

MOMENTUM IS BUILDING within K–12 education to redesign the traditional school day as a viable school reform strategy.[1] There is growing support within education circles to use *time* as an important resource for improving student learning outcomes in high-poverty schools.[2] Although there is no one uniform way schools use the extra hours, the most common models extend time devoted to the academic core subjects; expand learning time for all students in a grade level or across the grades, balancing academics, electives, and supplemental services; infuse enrichment and experiential learning via community partnerships throughout a longer learning day; or expand the school year, offering structured summer programs.[3]

The choice of one approach over another is context dependent, with each school[4] selecting a set of strategies that most adequately meet students' learning needs. However, all expanded learning strategies share a set of underlying beliefs: (1) a traditional school schedule is insufficient to prepare students for their postsecondary futures, (2) high-poverty students benefit from additional learning supports, and (3) time alone is not enough to change student learning outcomes; it is how that time is used that makes a meaningful difference in students' lives.

The purpose of this issue is to concentrate specifically on school–community partnerships through a blended construct, expanded learning time and opportunities (ELTO), whereby expanded learning time (ELT) schools work with community organizations offering expanded learning opportunities (ELOs) as equal partners to provide a seamless, longer learning day that best meet both the academic and developmental needs of students in resource-poor communities.[5]

ELT + ELO = ELTO

ELTO speaks to the centrality of school–community partnerships as a strategy to maximize staff talents and existing resources in a way that both addresses the learning barriers and opens students to engaging learning experiences.[6]

Why ELTO?

ELTO strategy promotes a balance among core academic subjects, electives, and developmental enrichment experiences. As a school reform approach, ELTO is designed to support closing of the achievement gap by expanding instructional time and elective offerings, and providing individualized tutoring and homework assistance, all of which have been demonstrated to result in higher scores on standardized tests and improved overall school performance.[7] As a youth development strategy, ELTO affords schools an opportunity to level the playing field for high-poverty students by exposing children and adolescents to enrichment and developmental opportunities routinely experienced by their wealthier counterparts, including music, arts and sciences, college preparation, field trips, service learning, internships, apprenticeships, recreational clubs, and interest-specific activities.[8]

ELTO partnerships bring together schools and quality community partners to join in programmatic planning and decision-making, service coordination, and knowledge-, data-, and resource-sharing. The ELTO partnerships thus often result in a shared vision, aligned goals, and joint delivery structures that provide students with enriching and engaging activities throughout a well-rounded learning day.

Although the school reform debate is often situated within the academic elements provided within expanded time schools, it is the

"O" in ELTO that offers new learning opportunities for students, opportunities that complement cognitive knowledge, build non-cognitive skills, and support students' individual goals.[9] These opportunities are often provided by quality community partners with a history of after-school and summer programs on local, state, or national levels. Although both schools and ELOs must agree to the contours of their partnership and how to sustain their joint efforts, the presence of community organizations within schools ultimately supports both partners and benefits students. Teachers gain flexibility in their schedules, extra help in their classrooms, and more time for professional development and common planning periods, and the ELO providers gain space, access to participants and to data systems, funding, and other resources that might not be readily accessible outside of the school context.

Contours of this issue

This issue makes the case for meaningful ELTO partnerships. The first half of the issue draws attention to the importance of ELOs in the expanded learning debate and offers contours of ELTO. The issue begins with two chapters devoted to making the case for the relevance of community partners in the expanded learning debate. The first chapter, "Expanded Learning Time and Opportunities: Key Principles, Driving Perspectives, and Major Challenges," by Dale A. Blyth and Laura LaCroix-Dalluhn, offers a theoretical basis for respecting and including nonformal learning opportunities in the expanded learning debate. Robert M. Stonehill, Sherri C. Lauver, Tara Donahue, Neil Naftzger, Carol K. McElvain, and Jaime Stephanidis present a policy case for the ELOs in "From After-School to Expanded Learning: A Decade of Progress," arguing that ELOs have for over a decade shown the value they add to student learning and achievement, and as such, should be elevated as integral features of school reform and improvement efforts.

NEW DIRECTIONS FOR YOUTH DEVELOPMENT • DOI: 10.1002/yd

The next two chapters focus on the school side of ELTO partnerships. In Chapter Three, "The Emergence of Time as a Lever for Learning," Christopher Gabrieli argues that ELT schools are an effective vehicle to help high-poverty students reach their academic potential and meet their developmental needs. Gabrieli suggests that ELT schools are a promising delivery mechanism for addressing whole-child needs in conjunction with teacher- and community-led enrichment services. The theoretical, first half of the issue ends with Chapter Four, "Expanding the Learning Day: An Essential Component of the Community Schools Strategy," in which Reuben Jacobson and Martin J. Blank compare and contrast the ELT schools with the community schools. The authors argue for the centrality of community schools strategy in the expanded learning discourse and offer a broader perspective on the importance of school-community partnerships.

The second half of the issue is dedicated to ELTO in practice, featuring a spectrum of ELT–ELO partnerships, ranging from less integrated (e.g., LA's BEST) to fully integrated (e.g., Citizen Schools) models. All models are designed to operate within an expanded learning time, to align with student learning needs, and to serve resource-poor, high-poverty neighborhoods. However, type of activities, uniformity of experiences, and the mandatory versus voluntary nature of ELOs in a given space vary and are based on the agreement with an individual school, school's learning goals and desired outcomes, stakeholder interests (principals, teachers, families, and students), and the available resources. The less integrated models offer out-of-school time, student-guided programs that meet a range of cognitive and noncognitive goals and maximize students' nonformal learning. Such partnerships offer participating students a variety of activities to choose from before or after school, on the weekends and/or in the summer, so there is no one uniform set of programs or experiences all students receive in a given school. The more integrated models, on the other hand, offer their services as course subjects during a longer school schedule, mandatory to students in a particular grade level or across an entire school.

NEW DIRECTIONS FOR YOUTH DEVELOPMENT • DOI: 10.1002/yd

The first example of a promising ELTO practice comes from Carla Sanger and Paul E. Heckman in "Expanded Learning the LA's BEST Way." Chapter Five offers a less-integrated ELTO model, LA's BEST, a values-based program-delivery system designed to meet children's developmental needs. LA's BEST partners with schools and offers experiential and enrichment opportunities outside of school hours, ranging from homework support to sports and interest-focused activities designed to encourage engagement in learning and noncognitive development.

The second model, ELT/NYC, is featured in Chapter Six, "The After-School Corporation's Approach to Expanded Learning." Anne-Marie E. Hoxie, Lisa DeBellis, and Saskia K. Traill make the case for ELT-ELO partnerships by guiding the reader through the development, refinement, and growth of ELT/NYC as a citywide expanded learning strategy designed to support schools' academic goals by utilizing the community organization's expertise in delivering innovative learning experiences to students as part of a longer school day. The seventh chapter features a fully integrated ELTO example, "Citizen Schools' Partner-Dependent Expanded Learning Model." Eric Schwarz and Emily McCann show how Citizen Schools, an ELO, has partnered with ELT schools across the country to work in concert with teachers and principals to offer students an engaging, academically focused learning day that produces improved student results.

The practice-oriented section concludes with Chapter Eight, "Building an Expanded Learning Time and Opportunities School: Principals' Perspectives," by the issue's editor, Helen Janc Malone. The piece is based on interviews with four ELT school principals across the country, who make the case for and offer the core features of their partnerships with ELOs. The issue concludes with Chapter Nine, "Next Steps in the Expanded Learning Discourse," by Helen Janc Malone and Gil G. Noam, who review the crosscutting themes, conceptual and practical challenges, and macrolevel steps to situate ELTO within the emerging education-reform debate on the use of expanded time as a viable youth learning and development strategy.

NEW DIRECTIONS FOR YOUTH DEVELOPMENT • DOI: 10.1002/yd

Conclusion

Improving high-poverty student educational outcomes and meeting developmental needs requires a whole-child approach to learning. Closing the achievement and opportunities gaps and helping students graduate from high school and go on to college or enter the workforce requires that stakeholder groups work collaboratively to create positive learning environments.

The expanded learning platform reimagines the school schedule, reshapes the roles and responsibilities schools have in resource-poor, high-poverty neighborhoods, and rethinks the relationship between schools and community partners. This issue illustrates one dimension of expanded learning strategy—the value community organizations bring to the school reform table, and the importance of committed ELT and ELO partners to create quality learning experiences for students. Because of the nascent nature of ELTO, data on the effectiveness of such partnerships and their link to student learning are still emerging; however, available evidence suggests that ELTO, when done with high fidelity, quality content delivery, and thoughtful implementation, can yield positive learning and developmental changes in students, which is the ultimate, desired goal of both stakeholders.

Helen Janc Malone
Editor

Notes

1. See National Center on Time & Learning and Education Commission of the States. (2011). *Learning time in America: Trends to reform the American school calendar—A snapshot of federal, state, and local action.* Boston, MA, and Denver, CO: Authors. Retrieved from http://www.timeandlearning.org /images/lta.pdf.

2. In 2011, there have been several bipartisan legislative opportunities to fund expanded learning strategies in K–12 schools, among them the Time for Innovation Matters in Education Act of 2011 (TIME), the School Turnaround and Rewards (STAR) Act, and the School Improvement Grants. There are also proposals on the Hill to expand the use of the 21st Century Community Learning Center program funds to include expanded learning time schools and full-service community schools.

3. Farbman, D. A. (2009). *Tracking an emerging movement: A report on expanded-time schools in America.* Boston: National Center on Time & Learning; Rocha, E. (2007). *Choosing more time for students: The what, why, and how of expanded learning.* Washington, DC: Center for American Progress; Remarks by the President of the United States to the Hispanic Chamber of Commerce on a Complete and Competitive American Education. (2009). Retrieved from http://www.whitehouse.gov.

4. School is defined in this issue as a K–12 traditional or charter institution, employing a number of strategies designed to boost student achievement and success, such as expanding the learning day and offering full-service community wraparound services, among a plethora of other strategies.

5. ELOs are defined in this issue as national, state, or local community-based organizations, intermediaries, or agencies that offer before-school, during school, after-school, weekend, summer, or year-round programs and/or services in partnership with a school, a cluster of schools, a school district, or in a community. ELOs offer nonformal learning programs that support a wide range of cognitive and noncognitive skill-building dimensions. ELOs could be voluntary or mandatory, depending on an agreement with a given education partner.

6. Although creating strong, quality education entails other dimensions— excellent teaching staff, strong principal leadership, sound curriculum, focus on instruction, and a data-driven culture—this issue is focused on the importance of including quality community partners in a longer school day to offer enrichment opportunities that enhance learning and development in students.

7. Frazier, J. A., & Morrison, F. J. (1998). The influence of extended-year schooling on growth of achievement and perceived competence in early elementary school. *Child Development, 69*(2), 495–497; The National Center on Time and Learning. (2011, Summer). *Learning time in America: Trends to reform the American school calendar.* Boston, MA: Author. Fountain, A. R., & Gamse, B. (2011, July 16). Evaluation of Citizen Schools' expanded learning time initiative. Presentation given at the Expanded Learning Time Summit. Boston, MA: Citizen Schools. Also see http://www.timeandlearning.org.

8. See, for example: Black, A. R., Doolittle, F., Zhu, P., Unterman, R., & Grossman, J. B. (2008). *The evaluation of enhanced academic instruction in after-school programs: Findings after the first year of implementation* (NCEE 2008–4022). Washington, DC: U.S. Department of Education; Lauer, P. A., Akiba, M., Wilkerson, S. B., Apthorp, H. A., Snow, D., & Martin-Glenn, M. (2006). Out-of-school-time programs: A meta-analysis of effects for at-risk students. *Review of Educational Research, 76*(2), 275–313; Vandell, D. L., Reisner, E. R., & Pierce, K. M. (2007, October). *Outcomes linked to high-quality afterschool programs: Longitudinal findings from the study of promising afterschool programs.* Irvine, CA, Madison, WI, and Washington, DC: University of California, Irvine, University of Wisconsin–Madison, and Policy Studies Associates, Inc.

9. Bowles, A., & Brand, B. (2009). *Learning around the clock: Benefits of expanding learning opportunities for older youth.* Washington, DC: American

Youth Policy Forum; Traphagen, K., & Johnson-Staub, C. (2010, February). *Expanded time, enriching experiences: Expanded learning time schools and community organization partnerships.* Washington, DC: Center for American Progress.

HELEN JANC MALONE *is an advanced doctoral candidate at the Harvard Graduate School of Education focusing on youth development and education policy research.*

Executive Summary

Chapter One: Expanded learning time and opportunities: Key principles, driving perspectives, and major challenges

Dale A. Blyth, Laura LaCroix-Dalluhn

This chapter emphasizes three key principles the education and youth development communities should consider in the current expanded learning debate: (1) respect the distinct differences and values of formal, nonformal, and informal learning, (2) acknowledge the value of a broad but clear definition and regular assessment of multiple elements of successful learning and development, and (3) reduce the current inequities in each approach to learning. The authors argue that students need exposure to both nonformal opportunities—after-school and summer programs—and informal learning—through family, peers, and community. Authors call for policy changes that recognize diverse forms of learning, encourage a wider set of measured outcomes within education, and broaden investments to cross both school and community boundaries.

Chapter Two: From after-school to expanded learning: A decade of progress

Robert M. Stonehill, Sherri C. Lauver, Tara Donahue, Neil Naftzger, Carol K. McElvain, Jaime Stephanidis

The authors examine the current expanded learning philosophical and policy debates, the impact of federal legislation on the debate between expanding versus extending the school day, and the

NEW DIRECTIONS FOR YOUTH DEVELOPMENT, NO. 131, FALL 2011 © WILEY PERIODICALS, INC.
Published online in Wiley Online Library (wileyonlinelibrary.com) • DOI: 10.1002/yd.404

important role expanded learning opportunities play as a promising school reform component. The authors suggest that expanding the learning day is best achieved through school–community partnerships that provide students a seamless day of academic and enrichment opportunities. The authors propose several policy recommendations: (1) promote a unified expanded learning vision, (2) implement a broad research agenda, (3) use existing funds strategically, (4) focus on improving staff quality and career opportunities, (5) support intermediaries, and (6) create and disseminate integrated models of school reform that include expanded learning opportunities as a primary feature.

Chapter Three: The emergence of time as a lever for learning

Christopher Gabrieli

Based on his experience with the Massachusetts Expanded Learning Time Initiative, the author argues that expanded learning time (ELT) schools are an effective education reform strategy that rethinks the outdated traditional school calendar by lengthening the school schedule and addressing a wider set of student learning needs. The author suggests that ELT schools are best positioned to provide both the academic instruction and youth development programs, often in partnership with selected, quality community partners. The chapter addresses partnership building, human capital concerns, costs and resources, and the future directions for this strategy.

Chapter Four: Expanding the learning day: An essential component of the community schools strategy

Reuben Jacobson, Martin J. Blank

Community schools are a decades-old strategy designed to integrate schools into their communities and to serve the whole child, family, and adults in the community. This chapter compares and contrasts community schools strategy with the expanded learning time (ELT) schools. The authors posit that community schools are an effective vehicle for implementing expanded learning time and opportunities in public schools. The chapter features several cases of successful expanded learning community schools and closes with a set of principles for using expanded learning in a community school setting.

Chapter Five: Expanded learning the LA's BEST way

Carla Sanger, Paul E. Heckman

Established in 1988 through a partnership between the City of Los Angeles and the Los Angeles Unified School District, LA's BEST presents an example of a community-based organization that collaborates with schools and other community agencies to create enrichment learning opportunities for low-income children and youth. This chapter highlights LA's BEST, a citywide after-school program that provides children and youth with enrichment experiences, academic support, recreation, and personalized student-guided learning. Authors describe the LA's BEST values-based program-delivery design and review the program's evaluation evidence of effectiveness. The authors conclude by urging policymakers to support programs that promote learning outside a traditional school day.

Chapter Six: The After-School Corporation's approach to expanded learning

Anne-Marie E. Hoxie, Lisa DeBellis, Saskia K. Traill

The After-School Corporation (TASC), a New York City intermediary, believes that by increasing the amount of time that they spend in school, students can participate in diverse activities that go beyond the structured school curricula. Although TASC continues to oversee dozens of quality out-of-school-time programs, the intermediary has launched in 2008 an expanded learning strategy, ELT/NYC. In this chapter, the authors lay out the research base for ELT/NYC, describe the implementation of the strategy, present emerging evidence of its success, and explain how the strategy helps to reform public schools to meet a range of student needs while supporting families, communities, and schools.

Chapter Seven: Citizen Schools' partner-dependent expanded learning model

Eric Schwarz, Emily McCann

This "how to" on school–expanded learning opportunities partner collaboration outlines lessons learned from over a decade of practice working in expanded learning time schools. Although Citizen Schools modifies its program model to accommodate schools, the organization also has specific optional and mandatory elements that give it flexibility while maintaining program quality and consistency. The authors describe key features of their partner-dependent model, including focus on planning, strong leadership, clear expectations, sharing data, and measuring success. Authors conclude that the best partnerships are where schools are reimagined, improving student results and experiences.

Chapter Eight: Building an expanded learning time and opportunities school: Principals' perspectives

Helen Janc Malone

Four veteran principals of Leo Politi Elementary School (Los Angeles), Jane Long Middle School (Houston), The Bronx School of Science Inquiry and Investigation (Bronx, New York), and Edward Bleeker Junior High School (Queens, New York) describe

NEW DIRECTIONS FOR YOUTH DEVELOPMENT • DOI: 10.1002/yd

the main considerations they had to balance when expanding the school day, among them time, teacher buy-in, community partnerships, developmental services for students, and family involvement. The principals note that expanding the instructional core alone is insufficient to meet the needs of their students. Given that a majority of their students live in resource-poor communities, the schools partner with citywide and nationwide partners in order to expose their students to enrichment experiences and developmental services. Emerging data suggest that their expanded learning strategy is increasing academic performance, school attendance, and student satisfaction.

Chapter Nine: Next steps in the expanded learning discourse

Helen Janc Malone, Gil G. Noam

This concluding chapter reviews the issue's crosscutting themes—focus on equity, quality use of time, stakeholder relationship building, and commitment to data. The chapter also addresses both conceptual and practical challenges facing ELTO and proposes three macro level steps for engaging expanded learning organizations in the national expanded learning discourse, including investing in a broader vision of expanded learning, focusing on comprehensive evidence-based strategies, and creating a unified advocacy message to sustain and grow funding streams that support quality learning experiences for children and youth.

*If expanded learning is going to make a real dif-
ference, then three key principles must inform how
communities overcome challenges and assure equitable access to learning opportunities.*

1

Expanded learning time and opportunities: Key principles, driving perspectives, and major challenges

Dale A. Blyth, Laura LaCroix-Dalluhn

A NATIONAL CALL to expand learning provides a chance to improve
the learning and development of America's children and youth, as
well as to transform the way Americans think about learning. To
make the most of this chance, three key principles should drive
change: respect the distinct nature and values of three approaches
to learning, acknowledge the value of an expanded definition of
success, and reduce the current inequities in each approach to
learning.[1] Analyzing the goals driving change today (and the real
benefits and distorting effect of each), the challenging nature of
today's schools, and the diversity and nonsystem nature of nonformal and informal learning opportunities is also critical. In the
midst of these realities and challenges there is hope that expanded
learning significantly increases the ability of all children and youth
to learn, lead, and contribute now, as well as prepare for work, college, citizenship, and life in the twenty-first century.

A combination of forces has led to a widespread call to expand
learning—from renewed commitment to address major

NEW DIRECTIONS FOR YOUTH DEVELOPMENT, NO. 131, FALL 2011 © WILEY PERIODICALS, INC.
Published online in Wiley Online Library (wileyonlinelibrary.com) • DOI: 10.1002/yd.405

educational disparities, to innovative educational improvement efforts, to the growth of after-school programs and increasing evidence of their impact.[2] These efforts were in part influenced by the report of The Time and Learning Task Force, which called for rethinking the ways in which learning opportunities come together to create youth success.[3] The public debate on how best to use any additional time and optimize the impact of learning opportunities for youth is vitally important. Extending time in school and expanding opportunities for learning through experiences after school or summer are especially important parts of that debate. Research has shown young people are better able to gain the skills, knowledge, and abilities they need when they have access to a broad array of learning opportunities and supports.[4]

Much of today's debate is framed in the language of formal education systems—students, classrooms, schools—even though part of the expansion seeks to engage a wider range of community and family partners. In this chapter, we focus on the broader community context—a context that includes opportunities offered at school and by school staff but also those supported by a range of nonprofit and for-profit organizations and agencies. Our primary focus is on how nonformal expanded learning opportunities are viewed and incorporated as part of this debate and their role in helping ensure youth succeed.

Principle 1: Respect the distinct nature and value of major approaches to learning

Our international discussions and work in Minnesota (see http://extension.umn.edu/youth/research/) led us to use more explicit language for different approaches to learning. Table 1.1 highlights three different approaches to learning, identifies systems and structures that support them, and defines their primary outcomes.[5]

People learn throughout their lives through experience-centered opportunities at home, with friends, and in the

Table 1.1. Delineating different approaches to learning

	Formal	*Nonformal*	*Informal*
Approach to learning	Learning is content centered.	Learning is youth centered.	Learning is experience centered.
Definition	Intentional instruction in a structured environment intended to produce academic development and resulting in a diploma, degree, or some form of certification where participation by the learner is generally compulsory	Structured and intentional learning opportunities where participation by the learner is generally voluntary and personal development is emphasized	Learning in everyday life; opportunities may or may not be intentional
Examples	K–12 education, higher education, or vocational education	Expanded learning opportunities such as after-school or summer programs, park and recreation programs, and various other forms of youth programs	Learning to cook with a parent, learning to fix a car with a neighbor, or visiting a library or museum
Primary outcomes	Learning the designated content as defined by the learning institution, passing grade levels, and graduating from high school	Learning the value of engagement for developing a sense of competence, confidence, connection, and the importance of self-efficacy	Learning the value of exploring and experiencing life

community. Alan Rogers, a European educator, refers to these experience-based approaches as informal learning opportunities.[6] It is through informal learning opportunities that young people learn what it means to be part of a family and learn about culture, character, and hard work.

Distinct from these are nonformal learning opportunities that approach learning by creating youth-centered learning experiences.[7] Such nonformal learning experiences are highly contextualized and tend to be designed for specific populations and to meet specific, often developmental, needs. High-quality nonformal experiences are intentional and structured to engage the young person.[8] This approach to learning generally occurs in settings such as youth development, after-school, and summer programs.

In contrast, formal learning opportunities are content centered and generally lead toward certification, such as high school graduation. Schools primarily provide formal learning opportunities, and the education system tends to make the decisions about what is taught, when it is taught, and who teaches it.

Although these approaches are conceptually distinct and typically occur in different settings, exceptional teachers, youth workers, and parents can utilize all approaches. Each approach brings specific types of intentionality, works best under certain circumstances, and is most likely to influence specific types of outcomes.

For example, developmental research identifies the need for young people to have choice over learning opportunities, participate in communities in meaningful ways, and gain self-efficacy to navigate the world around them.[9] These developmental needs are more likely to be met when young people have informal and nonformal opportunities to volunteer in their communities, participate in the arts, play sports, explore career options, and engage in the civic process. Furthermore, recent research shows that participation in high-quality nonformal learning opportunities not only supports developmental needs and social–emotional learning, but also contributes to success in other critical aspects of learning, such as grades, attendance, and test scores.[10] Yet too often the value and contributions of such programs are not well understood, and they are seen as nice, but not necessary.[11] These nonformal learning opportunities are increasingly essential in supporting a young person's achievement, and their absence is significantly responsible for disparities in academic success.[12]

In summary, this principle emphasizes the distinct value each approach adds to a young person's success. In a comprehensive and systematic effort, it is essential to expand not only time for each but also ensure each is done well. In short, this principle calls for expanded learning time and opportunities.

Principle 2: Acknowledge the need for and value of an expanded definition of success

This principle calls for measuring a broader set of outcomes at different ages to assure a young person is on course to succeed in his or her learning and development. For example, success could include measures related to readiness for kindergarten, reading by third grade, constructive engagement in nonformal learning opportunities, school attendance, contributions to family and community, and a sense of hope and self-efficacy.

James Heckman, an economist, raises a concern that much of the academic debate over success for youth is narrowed to gains in cognitive skills, which are commonly achieved through formal learning.[13] His research suggests that many of the skills and traits of successful individuals are noncognitive skills commonly acquired through nonformal and informal learning opportunities. Deborah Vandell, an early-childhood and after-school program researcher, shares a similar view. According to her research, young people reap the greatest benefit when intentional connections across cumulative learning experiences—at home, at school, and in the community—occur.[14] Narrowly focusing nonformal learning on improving test scores and grades is both less effective than a broader enrichment approach and is simply insufficient to prepare youth for success.[15]

A broad but explicit definition of success is critical to guiding the future development of comprehensive learning systems.[16] This principle becomes particularly important when the definition of success is combined with measurable indicators and calls for shared accountability.

Principle 3: Reduce inequities across diverse learning opportunities

Publicly recognizing the size, nature, and impact of current gaps in learning opportunities is also important. An opportunity gap is the difference between the availability, affordability, and accessibility of formal, informal, and nonformal learning opportunities. Families with means are purchasing learning opportunities for their children. They buy books, go to museums, and enroll their children in summer camps. These all contribute to learning outcomes and success in life.[17] By one estimate, a majority of academic differences in high school can be explained by differences in summer learning opportunities alone.[18] Children and youth who live in lower-income families and communities do not have the same access to these learning opportunities.[19] When it comes to nonformal learning opportunities in particular, America still allows separate and unequal systems to operate.

A recent statewide survey of parents and youth in Minnesota found that although families of different economic levels had roughly similar demands for nonformal learning opportunities, they had significantly lower access to a supply of high-quality, affordable, and accessible opportunities.[20] These data suggest that the differences in use of nonformal learning opportunities is less a demand problem and more a supply problem that will require community and system approaches.

Perspectives driving expanded learning

Public policy and resources for learning opportunities have traditionally been made available through state-funded formal education. Federal policies, such as Title I, are devoted to assuring equal educational opportunities among all children and youth. Until recently, there was limited public dialog about the importance of informal and nonformal learning opportunities and the role of communities in supporting parents. However, the passage of No Child Left Behind created a great deal of pressure on schools to ensure all children and youth are succeeding academically.[21] Although this has too often narrowed the focus to academic success, it has also increased recognition that such success also requires success in other domains. As schools across the country struggle to meet these expectations, however, most have recognized the need to expand the strategies they consider.

One strategy that garners a lot of attention is the amount and use of time for learning. In the report On the Clock, Elena Silva suggests that time alone is not the solution when striving to reach academic benchmarks; rather, it is the use of time that matters most.[22] Silva calls for an expansion of time to increase access to learning opportunities.[23] This section briefly describes three current perspectives and the goals driving them.

Goal 1: Improve academic achievement

Many schools across the country are extending time to improve academic achievement. The strategies employed often focus on extending time for content-focused formal learning and instruction.[24] The intentional use of time on instruction can support learning in focused areas.[25] The outcomes that result from these strategies are gains in specific cognitive skills and content knowledge.[26] In some cases, these efforts also include year-round schooling and rethinking summer as a time for learning.[27]

The problem of using academic achievement measures alone is that it distorts the ways different approaches are used. Although it can increase time on specific test-related learning tasks and encourages the use of data-based approaches to instruction, it also can simply extend formal learning approaches at the expense of nonformal learning approaches. These distortions are likely to make the nonformal approaches implemented less effective in supporting the overall success of young people and ironically, even less successful at contributing to academic achievement.

Goal 2: School improvement

The question of whether or not schools are effectively helping young people learn and succeed is another driving force today (e.g., U.S. Department of Education's School Improvement Funds, http://www2.ed.gov/programs/sif/index.html). Improvement efforts tend to concentrate on extending the school day or year, using data in decision making, or improving professional development.[28] Although worthy strategies, the school-centric language of the formal learning perspective too often underutilizes the distinct value of informal and nonformal learning approaches. Enrichment opportunities are often low on the priority list, too limited within the school, and offered by school personnel (rather than in partnership with community organizations).[29]

The results of such strategies have been mixed. Although there is considerable room and need for school improvement, it appears that such reform is less likely to transform the role of nonformal and informal learning opportunities fundamentally, to reduce inequities in these areas, and to engage their ability to support youth success significantly.

Goal 3: Strong community learning systems

Some efforts to support youth success are driven by a desire to increase the number of nonformal and informal learning opportunities in a community and their connection to schools.[30] When communities respond by providing such opportunities, both young people and their families feel supported.[31]

These efforts are often led by mayors in cooperation with schools and supported by an intermediary organization.[32] Communities using this approach are less likely to stimulate major school improvement, but more likely to build resources and supports for engaging youth in nonformal and informal learning opportunities (e.g., The After-School Corporation, New York, NY, http://www.tascorp.org; and After School Matters, Chicago, IL, http://www.afterschoolmatters.org). These citywide efforts have started to close the opportunity gap and have improved the quality of nonformal learning opportunities as well as academic outcomes.[33] They can create a stronger partner for the schools to work with rather than trying just to strengthen schools.

Challenges facing expanded learning efforts

Learning outcomes are highly interrelated, and it is the accumulation of learning experiences that lead toward long-term success.[34] The challenges facing expanded learning lie in the very nature of the main players—schools and the nonformal learning sector offering expanded learning opportunities.

Challenge: The nature of schools and school systems

Schools are generally looked to for solutions that incorporate learning outcomes because they are seen as the primary public investment in learning and as having the necessary infrastructure to do so systematically. Schools are often seen as "the only" consistent resource poor children can count on to help bring them out of poverty.[35] The fundamental nature of schools, however, creates challenges for expanding needed nonformal learning approaches.

Schools today are increasingly held accountable for an important but narrow set of academic outcomes that work against a broader definition of success and multiple approaches to learning. Schools also operate in a largely regulatory environment, whereas nonformal and informal learning often need a more incentive-based set of supports. There are also considerations given to transportation, data sharing, and other formal agreements when expanded learning opportunities are offered in schools. Naturally, the education system must be tapped as part of any new mix of expanded learning opportunities. The challenge lies in tapping into the best of what schools have to offer while also transforming them.

Challenge: Lack of coherent systems to support expanded learning opportunities

Although many community partners can contribute to a young person's learning, they typically are not coordinated or systematic in ways that allow policymakers to view the sector as a genuine part of the solution. The sector evolved into a nonsystem with multiple fiefdoms, few supports, and often, a more competitive than collaborative funding model that is short on stability and sustainability. Because of its nonsystemic nature and very different mix of funding (less public funding and more personal and private funding), it lacks a set of consistently measured and publicly reported outcomes and approaches to accountability.

Some questions exist regarding whether the nonformal learning sector can develop a systemic approach that is not at risk of evolving into a system that is too rigid and regulated. This is indeed a fundamental challenge for strategies that develop systematic data systems and schedules. Failure to address these challenges, however, is likely to perpetuate the inequities in learning opportunities that currently exist.

Promising policy directions

Two policy responses for addressing these challenges are worth noting. First, communities and states could establish a shared, broad set of outcomes for youth to guide public and private investments (for example, Change Makers in Action: Council for Youth Development, Columbus, IN, see http://forumfyi.org/files /Changemakers_Action_Columbus.pdf). These outcomes, periodically assessed and publicly reported, would allow policymakers and other funders to set more explicit, aligned, and less distorting long-term policy goals that generate new partnerships.[36] Second, the establishment of geographically defined regions for accountability that cross school and community boundaries could help to shift investments and improve outcomes. Policy shifts are unlikely in current times, but they may be exactly what is needed to create a successful, comprehensive approach to learning that honors the principles above.

Conclusion

This chapter reframes the expanded learning conversation by recommending three principles to drive efforts, recognizing the distorting effects of current goals, and finding ways to address the challenges that exist in both systems. Our hope is that the youth development field has the vision to support change, the wisdom to innovate, and the research to guide its future effectively.

Notes

1. We think successful youth are those who are ready for work, higher education, citizenship, and life. Success must include multiple cognitive as well as social–emotional indicators. Multiple, diverse, and engaging learning and developmental experiences at home, in the community, and at school provide youth with needed opportunities to gain the knowledge, skills, attitudes, and abilities they need to be successful.

2. Little, P. M. (2009). *Supporting student outcomes through expanded learning opportunities.* Cambridge, MA: Harvard Family Research Project.

3. The Time and Learning Task Force. (2007). *A new day for learning.* Washington, DC: Collaborative Communications Group. Retrieved from http://www.newdayforlearning.org.

4. Durlak, J. A., & Weissberg, R. P. (2007). *The impact of after-school programs that seek to promote personal and social skills.* Chicago, IL: CASEL, University of Illinois at Chicago.

5. Youth Community Connections. (2011). *Supporting youth success: The promise of expanded learning opportunities.* Minneapolis, MN: Minnesota's Statewide Afterschool Alliance. Retrieved from http:// www.youthcommunityconnections.org/PDF/SupportingYouthSuccess /MINNESOTA_FINAL_4.pdf.

6. Rogers, A. (2004*). Looking again at non-formal and informal education— Towards a new paradigm.* The Encyclopedia of Informal Education. Retrieved from http://www.infed.org/biblio/non_formal_paradigm.htm.

7. Rogers. (2004).

8. Durlak and Weissberg. (2007); Vandell, D., Reisner, E., & Pierce, K. (2007). *Outcomes linked to high-quality afterschool programs: Longitudinal findings from the study of promising practices.* Irvine, CA: University of California; and Washington, DC: Policy Studies Associates.

9. Konopka, G. (1973). Requirements for healthy development of adolescent youth. *Adolescence, 8*(31), 24.

10. Vandell et al. (2007); Alexander, K., Entwisle, L., & Olson, L. (2001). Schools, achievement, and inequality: A seasonal perspective. *Educational Evaluation and Policy Analysis, 23*(2), 171–191; Little. (2009); Stonehill, R. M., Little, P. M., Ross, S. M., Neergaard, L., Harrison, L., Ford, J., & Donner, J. (2009). *Enhancing school reform through expanded learning.* Naperville, IL: Learning Point Associates.

11. Heckman, J. J., & Rubinstein, Y. (2001). The importance of noncognitive skills: Lessons from the GED testing program. *The American Economic Review, 91*(2), 145–149.

12. Alexander, K. L., Entwisle, D. R., & Olson, L. S. (2007). Lasting consequences of the summer learning gap. *American Sociological Review, 72,* 176–180.

13. Alexander et al. (2007).

14. Vandell et al. (2007).

15. Heckman & Rubinstein (2001); Institute for a Comprehensive Workforce. (2010). *Expand options, expand achievement: How expanded learning options can reimagine education.* Washington, DC: U.S. Chamber of Commerce. Retrieved from http://icw.uschamber.com/sites/default/files/ICW_AFTERSCHOOL.pdf; Redd, Z., Cochran, S., Hair, E., & Moore, K. (2002). *Academic achievement programs and youth development: A synthesis.* Washington, DC: Child Trends; Russell, C. A., Reisner, E. R., Pearson, L. M., Afolabi, K. P., Miller, T. D., & Mielke, M. B. (2006). *Evaluation of DYCD's Out-of-School Time initiative: Report on the first year.* Washington, DC: Policy Studies Associates.

16. For an example see Piha, S., & the California Committee on Afterschool Accountability. (2006). *Holding California afterschool programs accountable.* Retrieved from http://www.cnyd.org/afterschool_outcomes.pdf.

17. Heynes, B. (1978). *Summer learning and the effects of schooling.* New York, NY: Academic; Entwisle, D. R., Alexander, K. L., & Olson, L. S. (2001). Keep the faucet flowing: Summer learning and home environment. *American Education, 25*(3), 10–15.

18. Alexander et al. (2007).

19. Heynes. (1978).

20. Lochner, A., Allen, G., & Blyth, D. (2009). *Exploring supply and demand for community learning opportunities in Minnesota: A survey of Minnesota parents and youth.* Minneapolis, MN: Center for Youth Development, University of Minnesota Extension.

21. Stonehill et al. (2009).

22. Silva, E. (2007). *On the clock: Rethinking the way schools use time.* Washington, DC: Education Sector.

23. Silva, E. (2007).

24. Boulay, B., Robertson, A., Maree, K., Fox, L., Unlu, F., Luck, R., & Gamse, B. (2010). *Year three outcomes report: 2008–2009 outcomes evaluation of the expanded learning time initiative final report.* Cambridge, MA: Abt Associates Inc.

25. Downey, D. B, von Hippel, P. T., & Broh, B. (2004). Are schools the great equalizer? School and non-school sources of inequality in cognitive skills. *American Sociological Review, 69*(5), 613–653.

26. Downey et al. (2004).

27. Entwisle et al. (2001).

28. Boulay et al. (2010); Stonehill et al. (2009).

29. Boulay et al. (2010).

30. CEOs for Cities. (2007). *CityTalent: Keeping young professionals (and their kids) in cities.* New York, NY: ForestCity Enterprises.

31. CEOs for Cities. (2007).

32. Bodilly, S. J., McCombs, J. S., Orr, N., Scherer, E., Constant, L., & Gershwin, D. (2010). *Hours of opportunity: Lessons from five cities on building systems to improve after-school, summer school, and other out-of-school-time programs* (Vol. 1). Santa Monica, CA: RAND Corporation.

33. Bodilly et al. (2010).

34. Vandell et al. (2007).

35. Neugro, P. (2009, January). *Expanding the concept of education.* Paper presented at the National Statewide Afterschool Network Annual Meeting. Clearwater, FL.

36. The Forum for Youth Investment. (2008). *Ready by 21: Changing the odds.* Washington, DC: Author. Retrieved from http://forumfyi.org /readyby21.

DALE A. BLYTH *is an associate dean at University of Minnesota and director of the Extension Center for Youth Development.*

LAURA LACROIX-DALLUHN *is the executive director of Youth Community Connections: Minnesota's Statewide Afterschool Alliance.*

NEW DIRECTIONS FOR YOUTH DEVELOPMENT • DOI: 10.1002/yd

*Following a decade of rapid expansion of after-
school enrichment programs, leaders in the field
are rethinking how those programs can be designed
to play a larger role in supporting student achievement and development and in strengthening school
reform initiatives.*

2

From after-school to expanded learning: A decade of progress

*Robert M. Stonehill, Sherri C. Lauver,
Tara Donahue, Neil Naftzger,
Carol K. McElvain, Jaime Stephanidis*

OVER THE PAST DECADE, expanded learning opportunities (ELOs) have begun to redefine the traditional boundaries between the school day and after school, and between the school building and the community. Despite variations in how ELO initiatives are designed and implemented, most share the common feature of cre-ating collaborative school–community partnerships that align aca-demic and enrichment activities to support student learning and growth, adding value to both in- and out-of-school time. At their best, ELOs incorporate experiential learning, civic engagement, career internships, leadership, mentoring, and other wraparound supports that schools alone may not be able to provide.[1] In fact, ELO advocates argue that the increased flexibility of ELOs permit staff to leverage a range of community resources to meet specific youth and community needs.[2]

NEW DIRECTIONS FOR YOUTH DEVELOPMENT, NO. 131, FALL 2011 © WILEY PERIODICALS, INC.
Published online in Wiley Online Library (wileyonlinelibrary.com) • DOI: 10.1002/yd.406

In the broadest definition, ELOs describe the range of student programs and activities that occur beyond the traditional school hours. ELOs appeal to a variety of student interests, blend the resources of schools and community organizations, and operate on a twenty-four/seven schedule: before and after school, weekends, evenings, and summers.[3] At a further stage of development, ELOs offer an emerging view of teaching and learning not limited by time or place.

Traditional after-school programs provide services during a set-aside period of time, whereas ELOs strive to integrate school and after-school time seamlessly to redesign a school's entire educational program.[4] In contrast, *extended learning time* is a term used to describe the lengthening of the school day, school week, or academic year to provide additional instruction in core academic subjects to enhance student success.[5] This chapter focuses on school-based programs, which often collaborate with community-based organizations that provide services at the school.

The drive to incorporate ELOs into school reform initiatives more deeply stems from the overwhelming number of schools— more than 30,000—that have failed to make adequate yearly progress (AYP) under No Child Left Behind. Policymakers, school personnel, parents, and taxpayers agree that the traditional school day itself cannot dramatically alter the academic trajectory of students at risk of school failure.[6] In response to these failures and to federal legislation, schools have considered how they might re-engineer the traditional school day to meet ever-growing academic demands.

ELOs, in their various forms, are gaining momentum as a key component of school reform, especially for low-income, high-risk students. They are also a fundamental component of promising charter-school models, including the Knowledge Is Power Program (KIPP), Achievement First, and Uncommon Schools.[7] A well-publicized example of expanded learning time and opportunities, the Massachusetts Expanded Learning Time initiative, developed a whole-school model of expanded learning in which twenty-six schools provided additional academic instruction and ELOs for all students.[8] The After-School Corporation (TASC) is implementing a similar initiative (though attendance is not compulsory) to more than 3,200 students in seventeen New York City public elementary and middle schools.[9] The C. S. Mott Foundation created A New Day for Learning initiative across ten U.S. cities to support ELO strategies that are "seamless and unrestricted by walls, clocks, or calendars."[10] These schools integrate academic instruction with arts, technology, service learning, and other services; encourage collaboration across sectors; and deliberately focus on students' development of twenty-first century skills such as critical thinking, problem solving, and teamwork. This chapter examines four aspects of the ELO movement: the current philosophical and policy debates, the impact of federal legislation, how expanded learning efforts are increasingly seen as a promising school reform component, and policy recommendations to support a national vision for expanded learning time and opportunities.

The current debate regarding expanded versus extended

Educators, policymakers, and funders have become somewhat divided over the future of the after-school movement. At the federal level, the U.S. Department of Education's (ED) ESEA Reauthorization Blueprint seeks to revise the purpose of the 21st Century Community Learning Centers (CCLC) program to authorize the use of funds for longer school days and community schools. Because lengthening the school day as a way to improve academic outcomes is a relatively new strategy in school turnaround, there is little research about the impact of longer school days on students. A recent review of research on extended learning time programs demonstrated that the research designs have been weak, so few conclusions can be made.[11]

In recent years, the issue of accountability relative to the funding of after-school programs has largely revolved around assessing the impact of these programs on student achievement outcomes. However, as noted by Robert Granger,[12] much of the research on the performance of after-school programs in supporting students' academic growth demonstrates an uneven level of effectiveness, with programs that provide higher-quality offerings tending to have significant impacts on student learning and others none whatsoever.[13] Generally, given the limited amount of time youth spend in these programs, a strong argument can be made that high-quality programs are most likely to have a relatively small but detectable impact on student achievement outcomes (effect sizes in the 0.05–0.10 range).[14] In the last decade, we have learned what components make a high-quality program, and we know that high-quality programs are more likely to lead to strong outcomes. In the Durlak and Weissberg meta-analysis, for example, programs with the greatest impact offered sequenced, active, focused, and explicit (SAFE) student activities.[15]

As another example of meaningful progress in uncovering what constitutes quality after-school programming, a number of recent efforts have used this knowledge about critical program components to develop quality assessment and improvement systems.[16] Effective quality-improvement systems are now the most pressing issue before the ELO community.[17] Several states, including Massachusetts, Wisconsin, New Mexico, New York, and Michigan, among others, now use observational tools and program-outcome data to guide specific program improvement strategies.

The research suggests a variety of paths that ELO programs can use to improve reading and mathematics outcomes.[18] Evidence-based strategies have included: improving youths' personal and social behavior through intentional methods with the use of the SAFE protocol;[19] delivering tutoring-like services and activities;[20] emphasizing skill building and mastery;[21] and offering explicit, research-based curricular models and teaching practices designed for the after-school setting.[22]

NEW DIRECTIONS FOR YOUTH DEVELOPMENT • DOI: 10.1002/yd

The impact of the American Recovery and Reinvestment Act on expanded learning time and opportunities

The American Recovery and Reinvestment Act (ARRA) provided approximately $80 billion to support educational initiatives. These dollars were delivered through supplements to federal funding streams such as Title I and IDEA, state fiscal stabilization funds distributed to governors, the Race to the Top (RTT) grants made to twelve states, and the forty-nine Investment in Innovation (i3) grants.

Other than the increase in child care and development block grant funds, nothing else in ARRA specifically supported ELOs. Nevertheless, nearly any ARRA funding stream can support ELOs as a component of a model to turn around chronically low-performing schools. Learning Point Associates has analyzed all of the RTT applications to assess how states incorporate after-school, expanded learning, and extended day language and strategies into their plans. Their preliminary review indicated that the RTT applications more often refer to after-school programs and extended day than to expanded learning, and most often in conjunction with programs targeted to science, technology, engineering, and math (STEM), twenty-first century skills, dropout prevention, and turnaround efforts. As can be seen in Table 2.1, states typically propose using RTT, Title I, and school improvement grants (SIGs) to expand the school day, largely through after-school programs, and to expand the school year.

The Round Two analysis explored how states were defining extended learning, expanded learning, and after-school learning in

Table 2.1. Use of extended, expanded, or restructured learning time in moving toward individual instruction

Number of applicants				Percentage of applicants			
Yes	*No*	*In progress*	*Planned*	*Yes*	*No*	*In progress*	*Planned*
9	12	2	18	22%	29%	5%	44%

NEW DIRECTIONS FOR YOUTH DEVELOPMENT • DOI: 10.1002/yd

Figure 2.1. Number of states referencing after-school, expanded learning, or extended learning in application

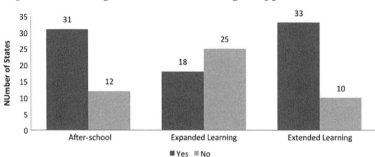

more detail. Figure 2.1 shows the number of states referencing after-school, expanded learning, or extended learning in their RTT applications.

Observations and trends

Although there were a variety of after-school, expanded learning, and extended learning strategies discussed throughout the applications, four prominent themes emerged in the analyses: a focus on older, high-risk students; STEM programming, teacher professional development to meet the demands of an extended school day: and recruiting community partners to help sustain the programs. Several of the states used after-school programming to target specific subpopulations of students, including those who were at risk academically or students who were English language learners (ELLs). (Note that the RTT applications reflect how states plan to incorporate ELOs, not how they are actually being implemented.)

Older, high-risk students

Lowering dropout rates and providing additional support to students in danger of dropping out was a common theme seen across the applications. For example, the District of Columbia plans to offer a Twilight program to accelerate credit accumulation for students who drop out for a short period of time but then return to high school.

STEM programming

STEM programming, especially for girls and low-income students in states including Delaware, were noted. Delaware plans to reach students who may not be familiar with science, math, or engineering curricula in six to eight low-performing districts.

Professional development for teachers to meet the demands of an expanded school day

Several states plan to use RTT funds to provide professional development for teachers; in particular, to help teachers understand how to make the most of the additional time and to incorporate enrichment activities to keep students engaged. For instance, Hawaii is planning an aggressive professional development plan for its teachers, including a 20 percent salary increase for a twelve-month contract.

Recruiting community partners to help sustain the programs

Across the applications, states discussed the community partners that were currently involved in their expanded learning initiatives. For instance, the Rhode Island Department of Education (RIDE) regularly works in close collaboration with a wide range of community, education, philanthropic, business, and civic leaders on issues related to student achievement.

Expanded learning time and opportunities as a promising school reform model

For more than two decades, a wide range of public and private funders have provided substantial investments to design, implement, and evaluate comprehensive school reform approaches in high-need, low-performing districts and schools. At the same time, the federal government and a range of philanthropies invested substantial resources to promote a more constructive use of students' time through after-school programs. To shine a spotlight on this issue, Learning Point Associates and the Collaborative for Building After-School Systems (CBASS) launched a national initiative in 2009 to better connect school-centered efforts to increase student achievement and those that employ student-focused interventions.

The group's report, Enhancing School Reform Through Expanded Learning, suggests ways in which school reform and improvement strategies can be complemented by activities designed to expand where, when, and how students can learn and grow.[23] In this report, a group of commissioned authors made an evidence-based case that:

- Expanded learning programs can be an effective strategy to promote student performance.[24]
- Charters were more likely than traditional public schools to incorporate additional time for learning as a key element of their philosophies.[25]
- Resources exist to enable districts and schools incorporate expanded learning activities as core components of their reform plans.[26]

In 2010, Learning Point Associates and CBASS issued a new policy brief: Integrating Expanded Learning and School Reform Initiatives: Challenges and Strategies.[27] The key research-based message of this initiative is that high-quality expanded learning can contribute to improved student achievement; however, after-school academic and enrichment programs are typically not incorporated as a core element in school reform efforts. And as noted earlier, the economic and political landscape changed dramatically in the past two years, with ARRA and other initiatives offering unprecedented opportunities—and imperatives—for collaboration.

NEW DIRECTIONS FOR YOUTH DEVELOPMENT • DOI: 10.1002/yd

Proposed policy recommendations

1. Engage school leaders and policymakers to develop a unified vision of expanded learning that clearly describes its core elements and defines reasonable impact indicators and appropriate outcomes. School reformers are only beginning to assess the value of ELO programs and their core elements as a cornerstone of their reform efforts. Engagement can occur through a range of activities and strategies, including a marketing campaign to brand ELO as part of new school reform models; an interactive Web site to build a community of professionals engaged in ELO models; and dissemination of evaluations of high-quality after-school programs that demonstrate significant, positive impacts on a range of outcomes.

2. Implement a broad research agenda around ELOs and their connections to school reform. A broad and rigorous research agenda is needed to convince policymakers of the value of ELOs. Rigorous, longitudinal research and evaluation studies will strengthen the case for high-quality models and lead to a better understanding of their relationship to student outcomes.

3. Provide technical assistance to school and community leaders seeking to leverage existing funding streams for ELOs. New federal funding initiatives offer an unprecedented opportunity to fund ELOs as part of a larger package of reform initiatives. The increased investment and attention to ELOs suggest that they are one of several promising mechanisms to advance meaningful school reform during the next decade.

4. Improve staff quality and career opportunities. Staff need the skills to provide programming to all students, as well as special skills in project-based learning, and an ability to use data to drive instructional supports. Attracting multi-talented people into programs that offer part-time employment and few benefits is a daunting challenge. In response, organizations such as the National After-school Association, the National Institute on Out-of-School Time (NIOST), and

TASC's Center for After-School Excellence have developed career pathway programs for youth workers who wish to earn college course credit or professional certificates. Several states offer school-age care credentials to individuals who participate in rigorous coursework and assessments, including portfolio review and on-site observation.

5. Support intermediaries that can promote high-quality ELOs. In the past decade, several organizations that provide communitywide training and technical assistance have played an increasingly important role in developing high-quality citywide ELO initiatives by raising awareness of the community's need for ELOs, developing varying models that appeal to students, sharing resources, and showcasing the successes of their programs with city and school officials.

6. Create, validate, and disseminate integrated models of school reform that include ELOs as a primary feature. Despite substantive investments, only some of the turnaround efforts designed to reform failing schools will achieve success. A careful study of successful, integrated school reform models employing ELO strategies will likely lead to clear lessons for school leaders and policymakers. Ultimately, the goal of ELO initiatives is a seamless integration with the tool kit of school-improvement strategies disseminated to school leaders.

Challenges

Now more than ever, neither schools nor out-of-school-time providers can afford to work independently of one another. As opposed to other polarizing reform initiatives such as performance-based compensation, high-stakes testing, or vouchers, expanded learning time and opportunities models are poised to receive strong backing from leadership of both political parties during the next reauthorization of ESEA. Schools needing to make adequate yearly progress under NCLB are more likely to seek successful after-school programs to enhance and promote students' achievement in core subject areas.

Supporters of ELOs can continue to track and influence how changes in education policy and funding opportunities promote expanded learning across various school contexts. Supporters should continue to urge policymakers and education leaders to offer funding to organizations that can identify, design, implement, and evaluate comprehensive school transformation models that incorporate ELOs. ELOs can complement, rather than replicate, the school day, if programs build strong relationships with their community partners. These partnerships ensure that youth have opportunities to participate in service learning activities, internships, and cultural events. Each of these activities help students gain real-world experience by providing them with authentic learning. Finally, educators, community members, and policymakers can work in partnership to understand the potential advantages that ELOs can bring to reform initiatives and support collaborative planning efforts at local and state levels.

Notes

1. Afterschool Alliance. (2010). *Expanding learning opportunities across the country: Embracing multiple approaches and funding sources.* Washington, DC: Author.

2. Bowles, A., & Brand, B. (2009). *Learning around the clock: Benefits of expanded learning opportunities for older youth.* Washington, DC: American Youth Policy Forum.

3. Bowles & Brand, 2009; Learning Point Associates and The Collaborative for Building Afterschool Systems. (2010). Integrating expanded learning and school reform initiatives: Challenges and strategies (policy brief). Naperville, IL: Learning Point Associates. Retrieved from http://www2.learningpt .org/catalog/item.asp?SessionID=869534&productID=310; Little, P. M. (2009). *Expanded learning opportunities—Pathways to student success.* Cambridge, MA: Harvard Family Research Project; National Education Association. (2008). *Closing the gap through extended learning opportunities.* (policy brief). Washington, DC: National Education Association; Traphagen, K., & Johnson-Staub, C. (2010). *Expanded time, enriching experiences: Expanded learning time schools and community organization partnerships.* Washington, DC: Center for American Progress; White House Task Force on Childhood Obesity. (2010). *Solving the problem of childhood obesity within a generation: White House Task Force on Childhood Obesity report to the President.* Washington, DC: Author.

4. Little. (2009); Rocha, E. (2007). *Choosing more time for students: The what, why, and how of expanded learning.* Washington, DC: Center for American Progress. Retrieved from http://www.americanprogress.org /issues/2007/08/pdf/expanded_learning.pdf; Traphagen & Johnson-Staub (2010).

5. Rocha. (2007).

6. Little. (2009).

7. Traphagen & Johnson-Staub. (2010).

8. Boulay, B., Robertson, A., Maree, K., & Fox, L. (2010). *Outcomes evaluation of the expanded learning time initiative.* Cambridge, MA: Abt Associates.

9. The After-School Corporation. (2010). *Re-imagining the 21st century school day—Expanded learning time.* New York, NY: Author. Retrieved from http://www.tascorp.org/content/document/detial/3104/.

10. C. S. Mott Foundation. (2010). *A new day for learning.* Retrieved from http://www.newdayforlearning.org.

11. Patall, E. A., Cooper, H., & Batts, A. (2010). Extending the school day or school year: A systematic review of research (1985–2009). *Review of Educational Research, 80*(3), 401–436.

12. Granger, R. C. (2008). After-school programs and academics: Implications for policy, practice, and research. *Social Policy Report, 22,* 3–19.

13. Durlak, J. A., & Weissberg, R. P. (2007). *The impact of after-school programs that promote personal and social skills.* Chicago, IL: Collaborative for Academic, Social, and Emotional Learning. Retrieved from http://www .pasesetter.com/reframe/documents/ASP-Full.pdf; Lauer, P. A., Akiba, M., Wilkerson, S. B., Apthorp, H. S., Snow, D., & Matin-Glenn, M. L. (2006). Out-of-school-time programs: A meta-analysis of effects for at-risk students. *Review of Educational Research, 76,* 275–313; Zief, S. G., & Lauver, S. C. (2006). *Impacts of after school programs on student outcomes: A systematic review for the Campbell Collaboration.* Philadelphia, PA: The Campbell Collaboration.

14. Kane, T. J. (2004). The impact of after-school programs: Interpreting the results of four recent evaluations. New York, NY: W. T. Grant Foundation.

15. Durlak & Weissberg. (2007).

16. Granger, R. C., Durlak, J., Yohalem, N., & Reisner, E. (2007). *Improving after-school program quality.* New York, NY: W. T. Grant Foundation; Little, P. M. D., Wimer, C., & Weiss, H. B. (2007). After school programs in the 21st century: Their potential and what it takes to achieve it. *Issues and Opportunities in Out-of-School Time Evaluation, 10*; Vandell, D. L., Reisner, E. R., Brown, B. B., Dadisman, K., Pierce, K. M., & Lee, D., et al. (2005). The study of promising afterschool programs: Examination of intermediate outcomes in year 2. Irvine, CA: University of California, Irvine. Retrieved from http://childcare.gse.uci.edu/pdf/afterschool/reports/PASP%20Intermediate%20Outcomes.pdf; Yohalem, N., Wilson-Ahlstrom, A., with Fischer, S., & Shinn, M. (2007). *Measuring youth program quality: A guide to assessment tools.* Washington, DC: The Forum for Youth Investment, Impact Strategies, Inc.

17. Granger et al. (2007).

18. Birmingham, J., Pechman, E. M., Russell, C. A., & Mielke, M. (2005). *Shared features of high-performing after-school programs: A follow-up to the TASC evaluation.* Washington, DC: Policy Studies Associates; Black, A. R., Doolittle, F., Zhu, P., Unterman, R., & Grossman, J. B. (2008). *The evaluation of enhanced academic instruction in after-school programs: Findings after the first year of implementation (NCEE 2008–4021).* Washington, DC: National Center for Education Evaluation and Regional Assistance, Institute of Education Sciences, U.S. Department of Education; Durlak & Weissberg. (2007); Granger. (2008); Lauer et al. (2006); Vandell et al. (2005).

19. Durlak & Weissberg. (2007).

20. Lauer et al. (2006).

21. Birmingham et al. (2005).

22. Black et al. (2008).

23. Stonehill, R. M., Little, P. M., Ross, S. M., Neergaard, L., Harrison, L., Ford, J., ... Donner, J. (2009). *Enhancing school reform through expanded learning.* Naperville, IL, and New York, NY: Learning Point Associates and The Collaborative for Building After-School Systems. Retrieved from http://www.learningpt.org/pdfs/EnhancingSchoolReformthroughExpandedLearning.pdf.

24. Little. (2009).

25. Ross, S. M., Potter, A., Pack, J., McKay, D., Sanders, W., & Ashton, J. (2008). Implementation and outcomes of Supplemental Education Services: The Tennessee statewide evaluation study. *Journal of Students Placed At Risk, 13*(1), 26–58.

26. Deich, S. (2009). *Using expanded learning to support school reforms: Funding sources and strategies.* Washington, DC: Cross & Joftus.

27. Learning Point Associates and The Collaborative for Building After-school Systems. (2010).

ROBERT M. STONEHILL *is a managing director at the American Institutes for Research.*

SHERRI C. LAUVER *is a senior program associate at Synergy Enterprises, Inc.*

TARA DONAHUE *is an evaluation and research specialist at Edvantia.*

NEIL NAFTZGER *is a senior researcher at the American Institutes for Research.*

CAROL K. MCELVAIN *is a principal technical assistance consultant at the American Institutes for Research.*

JAIME STEPHANIDIS *is a technical assistance consultant at the American Institutes for Research.*

NEW DIRECTIONS FOR YOUTH DEVELOPMENT • DOI: 10.1002/yd

Expanding learning time in schools by extending their schedules is a growing movement aimed at helping high-poverty students get stronger academic skills and enjoy a more well-rounded education and positive development.

3

The emergence of time as a lever for learning

Christopher Gabrieli

MORE SCHOOLS THAN ever are expanding their schedules beyond the traditional limits of six and a half hours a day, 180 days of the year. Schools serving predominantly high-poverty populations make up the vast majority of this emerging movement as they try to overcome the widespread failure of schooling to meet academic goals for high-risk students. Although raising academic achievement is certainly the single biggest driver of this wave, many participants are also motivated by the desire to provide a well-rounded education to all children and to address their broader social–emotional and twenty-first century skills needs. This chapter offers an overview of expanded learning time (ELT) schools and their relationships with community-based partners offering expanded learning opportunities (ELOs).

NEW DIRECTIONS FOR YOUTH DEVELOPMENT, NO. 131, FALL 2011 © WILEY PERIODICALS, INC.
Published online in Wiley Online Library (wileyonlinelibrary.com) • DOI: 10.1002/yd.407

Breaking through the school-schedule time barrier

The overwhelming majority of today's K–12 schools continue to operate on a 180-day school schedule, a minimum set during the progressive movement in the early twentieth century. Although this traditional schedule seemed adequate during much of the twentieth century, progress measured by academic tests and by high school and college graduation rates has plateaued for more than twenty years. Further, our changing global society requires a re-envisioning of the school schedule in order to help students acquire a broader set of skills and competences necessary to succeed in the twenty-first century.

In response to changing market demands, the private tutoring business and a vast array of after-school and summer programs have blossomed but are chiefly available to families with significant resources. More recently, to close the achievement gap and help all students be college/career ready, some pioneering schools are expanding their scheduled learning time by 25–30 percent and more. Their origins, goals, designs, and outcomes vary considerably, but together they offer a promising alternative to a limited, traditional school day complemented by whatever parents can find and afford to buy or access for their children.

The traditional school schedule has been under challenge by experts and reformers for at least thirty years. For example, the landmark 1983 report, A Nation At Risk, called for five cornerstone changes to American K–12 education. Whereas four of these recommendations have gained great traction, the fifth—changing the American school schedule—has not. The Schools and Staffing Survey (SASS) conducted by the federal National Center for Education Statistics shows very little movement in district school schedules across the country between 1999 and 2000 and 2007 and 2008 with a tight distribution around a mean of 6.7 hours per day for 179 school days per year.[1]

In 1994, the Congressionally mandated National Education Commission on Time and Learning delivered its report, the title of which, "Prisoners of Time," could not have been more emphatic in the issue. The report summarized in its letter of transmittal to Congress:

Time is the missing element in our great national debate about learning and the need for higher standards for all students. Our schools and the people involved with them—students, teachers, administrators, parents, and staff—are prisoners of time, captives of the school clock and calendar. We have been asking the impossible of our students—that they learn as much as their foreign peers while spending only half as much time in core academic subjects. The reform movement of the last decade is destined to founder unless it is harnessed to more time for learning.[2]

It is only in the last decade that a significant number of schools began to act on these recommendations. Given that these schools emerged in the context of far greater autonomy than is afforded by conventional district school settings and have blossomed as standards-based accountability solidified, one could reasonably speculate that both greater pressure to perform and greater opportunity to innovate were needed before schools could take the bold steps necessary to overcome the extraordinary inertia around the traditional school schedule.

Expanded learning time schools

Started in the early 1990s, the charter-school movement envisages experimental schools, moving beyond the design and operating constraints of traditional schools to identify new ways for public schooling to succeed for students. Of the nearly 1,000 schools across the country that the National Center on Time & Learning identified as ELT schools choosing to expand the learning day significantly beyond local norms as an explicit educational strategy, more than three-quarters are charter schools.

Several of the nation's most prominent and successful charter management organizations (CMOs) consider expanding their hours as a cornerstone of their design. There are now ninety-nine Knowledge is Power Program (KIPP) schools in twenty states and the District of Columbia serving over 27,000 predominantly high-poverty students. KIPP highlights five pillars of its core operating principles—high expectations, choice and commitment by students and faculty, principal autonomy, focus on results, and more time. KIPP students generally attend school for 50–60 percent more time per year, with classes running from 7:30 A.M. to 5:00 P.M. every day, selected Saturday mornings, and one extra month in the summer.[3] Likewise, a number of other leading CMOs, such as Uncommon Schools, Achievement First, YES Prep, and Aspire Public Schools, all explicitly incorporate significantly more learning time into their design and show evidence supporting their claim that their blend of innovations, such as more time, yields significant academic achievement gains for their students.[4]

Across the country, more than 150 district public schools find a way to go well beyond their host district's baseline schedule for learning.[5] The most visible district school cohort is the Massachusetts Expanded Learning Time Initiative, which currently includes nineteen schools and over 12,000 students at all grade levels. These schools show a wide range of academic results, including well-documented breakaway successes at the Edwards Middle School in Boston, the Kuss Middle School in Fall River, and the Hiatt Elementary School in Worcester. Since their inception, these schools show outsized growth gains on the state's value-added measures compared to the majority of poverty schools across the state.[6] Also, all schools are able to expand arts, music, drama, sports, and other enrichment opportunities dramatically.

The newest cohort of ELT schools are the over 700 turnaround schools participating in the federal government's push to change outcomes for the most persistently underperforming schools in the country. Utilizing a $3.5 billion funding to the Title I School Improvement Grant fund distributed through states, over 95 percent of these schools have selected one of the two models that under federal regulations must include "increased learning time."[7]

The approximately 1,000 existing ELT public schools are diverse in many dimensions, including the amount of time added to the traditional school day, which ranges from 10 to 60 percent of additional school hours per day and up to twenty or thirty extra days per year. District schools are more likely, compared to charters, to use staggered scheduling to achieve some of the expansion and are also considerably more likely to have only some of the faculty participating. Roughly half of these schools pay teachers more for their longer hours, whereas the other half recruit teachers at pay parity to nearby schools with shorter hours.[8]

Schools that opt into ELT overwhelmingly serve poor, minority, and English-language-learner students; however, they take different paths to help these students succeed. Many elementary schools add to the length of the core block periods, especially for literacy. At higher grade levels, the balance between adding to mathematics and literacy grows more even, and the use of more time for personalized student academic support beyond standard classroom instruction increases a great deal.[9] Together, these schools offer more time on task, personalized education, focused teaching, and as a result, a deeper engagement in learning.

The ELT schools movement overlaps with other movements that aim to provide more learning time and/or services to students and families. For example, the after-school movement is a robust, national, diverse field with thousands of participants serving large numbers of children. The primary distinction with ELT schools is that these schools expand learning time on a mandatory basis for students as part of the core public school schedule, whereas after-school programs are voluntary and often operate outside of the public school mandate and funding. Another overlapping strategy is community schools, generally defined to include schools that offer wraparound services beyond core education. While ELT schools offer well-rounded education to students, community schools additionally extend their wraparound services to families and community members.

Expanding learning as a youth development strategy

Achieving high levels of core academic skill is a crucial goal, but learning time can and should also be expanded to achieve developmental goals. The Massachusetts Expanded Learning Time Initiative's legislative language requires schools to provide plans that address both objectives, and the new federal guidelines for increased learning time (ILT) for turnaround schools similarly call for the added time for each of core academics, enrichment, and teacher time.

Given that many ELT schools serve predominantly high-poverty students with a limited access to after-school supports, most schools invest in electives, giving students choices to select subjects and activities from a variety of fields. Expanding not just the time but also learning opportunities opens the door for all students to find activities where they can flourish and adults to whom they can bond. Schools have the facilities and students are already there. Mixing the mandatory nature of school schedules with the elective spirit of effective enrichment means that every student has both the obligation and the opportunity to grow and learn broadly.

Children of all backgrounds, and particularly children of poverty, need social–emotional support as they grow and develop. Here again, ELT schools vary in their approach with some doing far more than others. One approach that many schools utilize is advisory time where students can address life issues in supportive contexts with teachers and small groups of other students.[10] Another is for schools to incorporate mental health and social work services and organizations into the facility and schedule of the school.[11] Finally, electives and the longer periods spent with teachers allow students to develop healthy relationships with adults.

Expanding learning time in partnership with expanded learning opportunities

Many schools see ELT as a unique opportunity to incorporate community partners and educators into the full life of the school.

All nineteen schools in the Massachusetts Expanded Learning Time Initiative choose to do this and illustrate many different patterns of partnership. The most common strategy is for a school to contract with a community or cultural organization to run one or more electives for students. In addition to bringing in their enthusiasm and expertise, the school gains scheduling flexibility, supporting goals such as teacher collaboration time, as teachers can meet while students participate in partner-led electives.

Some of the organizations involved in these partnerships have deep histories in after-school programming and have modified their structure to fit the schools' approach. Instead of taking an approach focusing on filling up a specified long period of time outside of school, they instead focus on providing their best single offering during a period or an hour of school time a day. Many other organizations partnering with ELT schools are not after-school providers, but bring unique skills to the task. For example, the Boston Ballet works with a group of students at Edwards Middle School in Boston and the Chamber of Commerce arranges mentors for students at Kuss Middle School in Fall River.

Schools work closely with their partners, sharing school-scheduled time and facilities and providing integration into the overall school work and information flow. They also expect the partners to learn and adhere to school policies on behavior management, grading, and information sharing. Partners who elect to participate gain guaranteed student populations, often much larger than they have experienced in voluntary after-school programs, and sometimes receive a share of the school's core funding. Schools gain unique expertise, enthusiastic community educator partners, and staffing efficiency and flexibility.

ELT schools are also aware that the need for child care and engagement does not end when the final bell rings. For example, Cityview Elementary School in Worcester, Massachusetts, sought out an arrangement to ensure high-quality after-school child care would be available to all of its families for the period from 4 to 6

P.M. each school day. In fact, Cityview would not have proceeded on converting to an expanded day without being sure that some families could also obtain after-school care at the school. At Roxbury Preparatory Charter School in Boston, the concern focused on summers. Roxbury Prep feels that its students can benefit from rich, engaging summer programming, and they raise money from philanthropy and use volunteers to help identify and place every one of their students into a wide range of local and out-of-area summer opportunities, such as sleepover camps in Maine and New Hampshire and the space camp in Huntsville, Alabama.[12]

Emerging frontiers and challenges

We are in the early innings of learning what can be accomplished by expanding school schedules beyond their traditional boundaries. There are a variety of ways to do this, ranging from small groups clustered by needs, skills, and learning styles to individual tutoring by teachers or community partners.

Another area is expanding the learning day versus the learning year. It is clearly more cost-effective per added learning hour to add to the day, because all resources go directly into student learning versus the overhead of bus rides, meals, administration, and so forth. On the other hand, summer learning loss is well documented, and summer seems to offer a time when a different balance between core academics and enrichment can comfortably be captured.

Finally, the role for adaptive software is a rapidly emerging frontier. Newly developed adaptive software—like the Rocketship charter schools in California or New York City's School of One—promises exciting opportunities to support student learning through approaches that adaptively match challenge levels to each student's capability level, allow multiple approaches for students to learn material, have no time or location limits, and allow students to pursue their own interests.

NEW DIRECTIONS FOR YOUTH DEVELOPMENT • DOI: 10.1002/yd

Human capital and effective data use as necessary companions for success

No one can or should label ELT schools as a "silver bullet" panacea that in and of themselves ensure students reach high academic standards and enjoy a well-rounded education. On the other hand, the wide prevalence of this strategy at the most effective charter schools and at a growing number of improving district schools supports[13] the view that expanding time is necessary but not sufficient.

Qualitative research on effective ELT schools reveals essential companion practices found at successful schools.[14] First and foremost, success depends on effective leadership and teaching. For principals, this is both a tremendous opportunity and a clear test of their skills—from designing the overall program to including the teachers, students, and community effectively, to balancing between students' needs for stronger core academics and a well-rounded education, to managing new autonomies and resources. For teachers, it is an opportunity to spend more time improving their craft, developing new practices, and working with their colleagues in honing them.[15]

A second major cofactor for success is the use of data to drive instruction. More learning time creates opportunities to vector effective, personalized supports to every student, but doing so requires a frequently refreshed, accurate picture of where each student stands. Not only do such approaches allow powerful customization for students, but they also support teacher collaboration and coaching that focuses on the specific topics where students need different, more effective teaching.

Costs and resources

How much does it cost to expand a learning day in schools, and how can resources best be used in pursuing that approach? The majority of charter schools pay teachers no more than nearby schools with shorter hours and report little difficulty in finding teachers who want the high-energy, high-expectations environment they believe they offer as an alternative. Other charters offer stipends. In Massachusetts, the ELT schools receive $1,300 per student for 300 more hours and generally pay participating teachers on an hourly or percentage basis, based on each district's collective bargaining agreement process.[16]

Green Dot schools, currently located in Los Angeles and New York City, offer another model. These schools have collective bargaining agreements but do not specify the length of the day. They eliminate the concept of negotiated work hours and substitute the concept of the "professional day," which is defined to include the needed classroom, student support, and collaboration and planning time for teachers, as determined by consensus decision-making at the school. Teachers get paid somewhat more at these schools to enable both higher pay and more learning time.[17]

Although much remains to be determined in the future, it seems likely that the growing wave of ELT schools will draw their resources from a mix of reallocating current funds, accessing new federal, state, and local funds dedicated to expanded time and novel arrangements with teachers and community partners that compensate them for their efforts and hours.

The future

ELT schools go beyond the standardized, assembly-line school model. Pioneering models show that schools, together in many cases with ELOs, can offer a better way, expanding both the learning time and opportunities. The most impressive of these schools are posting important academic results, with students vastly outperforming the dismal outcomes normally expected from students of high poverty and other disadvantages.

The next decade is likely to see the growth of ELT schools. However, the ultimate shape of schools and education as learning becomes more personalized and variable is yet to be determined.

As Carnegie units of seat-time yield ever more to measures of mastery not bound by time (or place), we are likely to see all schools gain a more Montessori-like blending of ages, levels, and approaches. Adaptive software is likely to gain a significant role with teachers more focused on personalization and interaction. In the end, it is hard to see how we can ever end up any place other than seeing that each child needs and deserves the learning time and opportunities that fits their unique situations. When "schools" can offer this to all of our students, especially our most disadvantaged, then truly we can see that we have matched learning time to learning need. Nothing less should be acceptable.

Notes

1. Kolbe, T., Partridge, M., & O'Reilly, F. (2011). *Time and learning in schools: A national profile*. Storrs, CT, and Boston, MA: National Center on Time and Learning and Center for Education Policy Analysis at University of Connecticut.

2. National Education Commission on Time and Learning. (1994, April). *Prisoners of time*. Report of the National Education Commission of Time and Learning. Washington, DC: U.S. Government Printing Office.

3. Knowledge Is Power Program. (n.d.). *KIPP five pillars*. Retrieved from http://www.kipp.org/about-kipp/five-pillars.

4. National Alliance for Public Charter Schools. (2010*). Measuring charter performance: A review of public charter school achievement studies*. Washington, DC: National Alliance for Public Charter Schools.

5. Farbman, D. (2011). *Leveraging more time to improve schools: A study of three districts*. Boston, MA: National Center on Time and Learning.

6. Data can be accessed at http://profiles.doe.mass.edu.

7. National Archives and Records Administration Office of the Federal Register (2009). Federal Register (74 FR 59805). Washington, DC: U.S. Government Printing Office.

8. Farbman, D. (2009). *Tracking an emerging movement: A report on expanded time schools in America*. Boston, MA: National Center on Time and Learning, p. 17.

9. Farbman. (2009).

10. Gabrieli, C., & Goldstein, W. (2008). *Time to learn: How a new school schedule is making smarter kids, happier parents, and safer neighborhoods.* (p. 106). San Francisco, CA: John Wiley and Sons.

11. City Connects. (n.d.). *Welcome to City Connects*. Retrieved from http://www.bc.edu/schools/lsoe/cityconnects/.

12. Roxbury Preparatory Charter School. (2009). *Preparing students for college and beyond—2008–2009 Annual Report*. Roxbury, MA: Roxbury Preparatory Charter School.

13. Data can be accessed at http://profiles.doe.mass.edu.

14. Gabrieli, C. (2010). More time, more learning. *Educational Leadership*, 67(7), 38–47.

15. Rivkin, S. G., Hanushek, E. A., & Kain, J. F. (2005). Teachers, schools, and academic achievement. *Econometric Society*, 73(2), 417–458; Darling-Hammond, L., Bransford, J., LePage, P., Hammerness, K., & Duffy, H. (Eds.). (2005). *Preparing teachers for a changing world: What teachers should learn and be able to do.* San Francisco, CA: Jossey-Bass Publishers.

16. Farbman. (2009).

17. Green Dot Public Schools. (n.d.). *Driving reform.* Retrieved from http://www.greendot.org/driving_reform; Annenberg Institute for School Reform. (2008). *Green Dot Schools site profile 2008: Green Dot public schools and Los Angeles parents union.* Providence, RI: Annenberg Institute for School Reform at Brown University. Retrieved from http://www.annenberginstitute.org/pdf/EKF08_GreenDot.pdf.

CHRISTOPHER GABRIELI *is chairman of the National Center on Time & Learning and an adjunct lecturer at the Harvard Graduate School of Education.*

NEW DIRECTIONS FOR YOUTH DEVELOPMENT • DOI: 10.1002/yd

Community schools expand learning time and opportunities as one important dimension of a comprehensive strategy to ensure that students are ready for college, career, and citizenship.

4

Expanding the learning day: An essential component of the community schools strategy

Reuben Jacobson, Martin J. Blank

FROM THEIR BEGINNING, community schools have expanded the learning day as a central component of their comprehensive strategy. Community schools of the early twentieth century served as centers of the community where students, families, and community members came to learn, to become civically engaged, and to prepare for the workforce. Students and families learned not only during traditional school hours, but also before and after the school bell rang, on weekends, and during breaks. In this way, community schools served as a precursor to current efforts to expand learning time and opportunities in schools. In both strategies, the school is viewed as the primary place for more learning time, more engagement, and more opportunities to improve life outcomes. However, in community schools, learning is linked to the community as well. Today, community schools and their partners continue to expand learning time and opportunities as one important dimension of a comprehensive strategy to ensure that

NEW DIRECTIONS FOR YOUTH DEVELOPMENT, NO. 131, FALL 2011 © WILEY PERIODICALS, INC.
Published online in Wiley Online Library (wileyonlinelibrary.com) • DOI: 10.1002/yd.408

students are ready for college, career, and citizenship, and to strengthen families and the community.

Much of the education literature recognizes that strong partnerships with community members, community-based organizations (CBOs), institutions of higher education, and agencies across sectors are critical in developing quality and sustainable expanded learning opportunities (ELOs).[1] However, expanded learning programs are faced with a number of challenges, including staffing, financing, developing partnerships, and family schedules that can be addressed by using the community school strategy. From our experience, the community school strategy is the vehicle for ensuring that partnerships are sustainable and support high-quality expanded learning time and opportunities.

In this chapter we describe community schools, lay out the similarities and differences between the community schools and the ELT schools, and provide examples of how community schools are expanding both learning time and opportunities. Finally, we present a set of principles for using expanded learning in a community school setting.

What is a community school?

According to the federal definition, a community school is both a place and a set of partnerships between the school and other community resources. It provides academics, health and social services, youth and community development, and community engagement, and brings together many partners to offer a range of support and opportunities for children, youth, families, and communities.[2]

Community schools improve student learning, strengthen families, and build healthier communities.[3] Community schools are not a program or model but rather a strategy for mobilizing school and community resources toward fulfilling the following conditions for learning:

- Early-childhood development programs nurture growth and development

- Students are motivated and engaged in learning—both in school and in community settings, during and after school
- The school has a core instructional program with qualified teachers, a challenging curriculum, and high standards and expectations for students
- The basic physical, mental, and emotional health needs of young people and their families are recognized and addressed
- There is mutual respect and effective collaboration among parents, families, and school staff
- Community engagement, together with school efforts, promotes a school climate that is safe, supportive, and respectful and that connects students to a broader learning community

Regular public schools, charter schools, magnet schools, alternative schools, and other types of schools all can be community schools.

In a fully developed community school, a school site team—including the principal, staff, community-school coordinator, family and community members, CBOs, and other school partners—is responsible for the planning and implementation of the strategy. It selects which results the school wants to achieve for students, families, and the community. The team ensures that community-school activities are aligned with instruction and other school reform strategies to achieve the identified results. The site team mobilizes local resources and captures local, state, and federal funds to finance the school's activities.[4]

In systems of community schools, an intermediary organization—a school district, nonprofit, or institution of higher education—supports the school site and coordinates the work of the community leadership team, which includes the school district, local government, higher education, community organizations, and parent and community organization leaders. The community leadership group is responsible for the overall vision and strategy.[5]

The rise of community schools and their support from U.S. Secretary of Education Arne Duncan suggests that local leaders are overcoming traditional barriers to community partnerships such as differences in culture, an emphasis on different results, and the complexity of federal and state funding streams. Several bills pending in Congress would further reduce these barriers. Community schools are growing because they are increasingly viewed as an efficient and effective use of scarce resources and provide a sustainable approach to creating partnerships that support student success.

As suggested earlier, community schools expand learning time and opportunities. The Center for American Progress (CAP) defines an ELT school as one engaged in "lengthening of the school day, school week or school year for all students in a given school" with the purpose "to focus on core academics and enrichment activities to enhance student success."[6] We share CAP's emphasis on enrichment opportunities, and strongly support connections to the core curriculum; we also encourage learning that exposes young people to new experiences and that develops their talents at all hours of the day.

Points of similarity between community schools and ELT schools

The expanded learning field shares a number of features that are similar to the broader community school strategy.

Expanded learning time

The most obvious similarity is that both reform strategies expand learning time for students. A central community school tenet is that schools become centers of the community and are open to everyone twenty-four/seven. Almost all community schools have after-school programming led by community partners.

Central to the school's reform strategy

Community schools and ELT schools change the way traditional schools do business. They are not add-ons to the long list of programs and interventions that educators must incorporate;[7] rather, both strategies are central to the school's overall reform agenda. In both types of schools, the work of community partners is integral to the school's improvement plan and aligned with the curriculum.

Local decision making

Both community school and ELT advocates argue that decisions about using either strategy should be made locally.[8] The differences are that in the community school strategy, a broader range of partners are engaged in the decision-making process; that a community leadership group considers ELT only in the context of multiple other strategies; and that local decision making is an essential principle of the strategy. In contrast, local decision making is suggested, but not required, of ELT schools.

Points of difference between community schools and the ELT schools

Because ELT is only one aspect of the community school strategy, there are also differences between the two.

More than learning

Most importantly, community schools are broader in purpose. They work to reduce barriers to learning by providing medical, dental, mental health, and social services; adult education; job training; community building; parent leadership and education; early-childhood programs; and other kinds of youth development. Schools are uniquely positioned in communities to offer these supports along with partners because they are the most visible and centrally located public institution that is able to reach students, families, and community members.

Expanded learning opportunities, not just time

Community schools expand learning through a variety of strategies, including after-school enrichment, tutoring, mentoring, community service, apprenticeships, and internships. These activities may occur outside of traditional school time, but they may also occur during the school day, in collaboration with community partners.

More than students

Although ELT schools focus their strategy on increasing learning time only for students, community schools provide more learning time for students, families, and community members. As centers of the community, community schools offer a place for families and communities to engage in multiple learning opportunities that meet local needs, such as learning English, job skills, and parenting skills. When students, families, and the community are learning in the same space, a school builds a community where learning becomes a prominent shared value.

Centrality of partners

Community schools recognize that school and community resources are essential to expanded learning, especially during challenging economic times, when school budgets cannot fund additional learning opportunities. Although the literature on ELT schools suggests partnerships, they are not required.[9] In contrast, a core principle of the community school strategy is that strong partners share resources, expertise, and staff when working with schools. Partners also participate in school decision-making processes.

Cases

In the community school setting, expanding the learning day can be characterized across four time dimensions: longer day, longer week, longer year, and summer school. A few examples illustrate the nature of how community schools implement expanded learning across these dimensions.

Longer day

When Young Achievers Science and Mathematics Pilot School in Boston, a 2010 federal Full Service Community School grantee, was founded over fifteen years ago, part of the founders' vision was to work with partners in supporting children beyond the traditional school hours.[10] The school expanded the day and offered programs before and after school, on Saturdays, and during the summer. With the expanded time, Young Achievers also provides expanded learning opportunities that support core academics.

Bwanda Owen, Director of School and Community Partnerships, works with the school's principal, academic coordinator, and after-school coordinator. Together, they make up the Extended Learning and Enrichment Team that meets once a week. Owen and the team identify the school's needs and work with the school's community partners to support expanded learning opportunities (ELOs) throughout the day, during the weekend, and over the summer. According to Owen, if Young Achievers were not a community school they would:

[P]robably be leaning more towards just trying to do everything ourselves, which doesn't work. It's really hard to have an extended learning program without the support of the partnerships and without the support of the community because it's really hard to have all these different enrichment activities just relying on the teachers.[11]

Longer week

Baltimore City Public Schools has a community schools initiative in twenty schools. Guilford Elementary Community School expands learning time during the weekend for targeted students who need additional support. However, after improving its test scores, Guilford Elementary lost its Supplemental Education Services funding that paid for ELOs. Guilford's leadership recognized that ELOs were critical to their success and looked to their community school partners to support their activities. One of many partners that answered the call was Camp Achieve, an ELO that emphasizes mathematics. Every other Saturday, Camp Achieve provides an additional three hours of mathematics instruction. Afterward, students apply the morning's mathematics lessons during a field trip. While students are receiving morning instruction, their parents participate in relevant learning opportunities such as financial literacy classes. Shana McIver, the Community School Resource Director, is central to coordinating the school's many expanded activities. Her position and the participation of community partners allow the staff to focus on their primary mission, instruction during the traditional school day. McIver bridges instruction with expanded activities so that participating community school partners support student learning.[12]

Longer year

Burroughs Elementary School, one of Chicago Public Schools' 150 community schools, underscores the importance of parental engagement to both strategies.[13] Burroughs' lead partner is the Brighton Park Neighborhood Council, which coordinates mental health, adult education, and other programming and services. Nearly eight years ago, Principal Richard Morris worked with his staff to lengthen the school day. Morris told his teachers that he thought they were doing students a disservice by not providing more learning time. Parents supported this notion.

Parents decided that they wanted the school to become a Track E school, meaning that the school year would start earlier in the summer, that there would be a two-week intersession in fall, and longer winter and spring breaks. Although intersession programs during the longer breaks are optional, Morris claims that attendance is nearly the same as regular school days.[14] Consequently, intersessions have increased the number of hours students are engaged in learning. Community partners operate their community school activities during intersessions just as they would during the traditional school calendar. Parents want their children to attend intersessions and students want to attend as well. In this way, Burroughs is open year-round to all students who are engaged in a real-world curriculum, supported by community partners.

A few community schools in the Tulsa Area Community Schools Initiative (TACSI), a system of eighteen community schools, operate on a similar extended-year schedule. Kendall-Whittier Elementary School addresses summer learning loss and creates more opportunity for students by adding twenty additional days of instruction for participating students during the intersessions, with an additional sixteen days for those who also participate in summer school. At Kendall-Whittier, parents, community members, and staff made the decision to utilize both the ELT and community school strategies. As principal Judy Feary said:

One of the things the neighborhood wanted was extended learning time for their children . . . And my staff wanted additional time for professional development. We knew we needed early childhood services, we knew we needed social services. The extended calendar would give us the opportunity to implement all these things.[15]

Summer school

Cincinnati provides an illustration of how a district strengthened expanded learning during the summer by taking a traditional summer school program to the next level with community partners to improve results for children. In Cincinnati Public Schools (CPS), schools are implementing the community school strategy to some degree.[16] In 2009, Superintendent Mary Ronan announced her plan to turn around the lowest-performing elementary schools. Community partners immediately organized to plan new summer learning opportunities. The new initiative was called the Fifth Quarter, and it emphasized the environment and real-world problem solving. In the morning, all Fifth Quarter schools focus on reading, English language arts, and mathematics. Community and school site teams decide what content and activities to offer during periods of enrichment in the afternoon and after school.

The Fifth Quarter has made an impact in CPS. The summer prior to its inception the traditional summer school program only attracted approximately 750 students across the sixteen schools. The Fifth Quarter now attracts nearly 2,500 students, or over 40 percent of enrolled students in the sixteen schools. Community schools that collaborated with more partners were able to recruit more students to participate. Being a community school was essential to this strategy. As Rebecca Kelley, Executive Director of Community Services YMCA of Greater Cincinnati, a CPS partner, explained:

Looking at cradle to college to career just cannot be done with the school resources alone, in terms of the breadth, depth, and level of excitement and positivity that comes from the community partners to serve young people and to help our community grow.[17]

Principles for using expanded learning time and opportunities in a community school setting

Overall, we suggest that any school considering expanding learning start with implementing the community school strategy, which provides the structure, partnerships, and resources that are helpful to embedding a new program into a comprehensive school strategy. We draw the following principles for such community schools.

First, decisions about how to incorporate longer hours into the school should be made jointly by school and community leadership. If expanding the school day does not work for parents, for teachers, or for community partners in a particular locality, it should not be implemented. A recent report argues that school districts that want to use community resources to increase learning time lack the capacity to develop and manage partnerships.[18] Community schools serve as the vehicle for engaging the community in designing quality ELOs. From a policy perspective, all levels of government should provide incentives for places that use results-driven public/private partnerships that support expanded learning and other activities.

Second, learning experiences must be enriching for students and be aligned with and strengthen the curriculum; expanded time must help motivate students to learn. The literature is clear—more time cannot mean more of the same.[19] Community schools and

ELT schools should use community resources to enhance and support the curriculum in ways that motivate students to take ownership of their learning.

Third, expanding the learning day must be a sustainable part of a broader comprehensive results-based strategy to improve student outcomes. Community schools plan their activities and services based on the results they want to achieve for students, families, and the community. If a partner, program, or strategy is not aligned with these results, it should not be considered. Community schools are more than a collection of community partners; partners collaborate with the school on multiple programs and services that support the school's results framework. Community schools sustain their activities through a variety of sources and any activities that are part of the larger community school strategy must have a sustainability plan.

Fourth, families, communities, and partners must be involved in decisions about expanded day development, particularly when formal extension of the day may affect the needs of working families and disrupt students' access to quality after-school opportunities. As the above points make clear, all decisions about time should be based on local context.

Conclusion

This volume is timely, as both ELT schools and community school strategies are garnering increased attention from policymakers and stakeholders.[20] From a community school perspective, policymakers, educators, and community leaders should start implementing expanded learning by creating the community school leadership structures that identify the results a community wants to achieve,[21] the resources available, and the activities that will best help achieve those results.

Notes

1. Rocha, E. (2007). *Choosing more time for students: The what, why, and how of expanded learning*. Washington, DC: Center for American Progress;

Stonehill, R., Donner, J., Morgan, E., & Lasagna, M. (2010). *Integrating expanded learning and school reform initiatives.* Naperville, IL, and New York, NY: Learning Point Associates and The Collaborative for Building After-School Systems; Traphagen, K., & Johnson-Staub, C. (2010). *Expanded time, enriching experiences: Expanded learning time schools and community organization partnerships.* Washington, DC: Center for American Progress.

2. U.S. Department of Education. (2009). *Title I guidelines.* Retrieved from http://www2.ed.gov/policy/gen/leg/recovery/guidance/titlei-reform .pdf.

3. See http://www.communityschools.org/results/overview.aspx.

4. A recent study found that a typical community school leverages a minimum of $3 for each $1 of school funds invested. Blank, M. J., Jacobson, R., Melaville, A., & Pearson, S. S. (2010). *Financing community schools: Leveraging resources to support student success.* Washington, DC: Institute for Educational Leadership.

5. Blank et al. (2010). This report also provides details on how community schools are organized and financed.

6. Rocha. (2007). P. 2.

7. Rocha. (2007).

8. Rocha. (2007); Blank, M. J., Berg, A. C., & Melaville, A. (2006). *Growing community schools: The role of cross-boundary leadership.* Washington, DC: Coalition for Community Schools.

9. Farbman, D. A. (2009). *Tracking an emerging movement: A report on expanded-time schools in America.* Boston: National Center on Time & Learning. Retrieved from http://www.timeandlearning.org/images/12.7.09FinalDa tabaseReport.pdf.

10. For more information, see http://www.youngachieversschool.org.

11. Owen, B. (director of school and community partnerships Young Achievers Science and Mathematics Pilot School). (2010, December). Personal communication.

12. McIver, S. (community school resource director at Guilford Elementary Community School). (2010, December). Personal communication.

13. For more information, see http://www.cpsafterschool.org/program.

14. Morris, R. (principal of Burroughs Elementary School). (2010, December). Personal communication.

15. Feary, J. (principal of Kendall-Whittier Elementary School). (2010, December). Personal communication.

16. For more information, see http://www.cps-k12.org/community/CLC /CLC.htm.

17. Kelley, R. (executive director of community services, YMCA of Greater Cincinnati). (2010, December). Personal communication.

18. Stonehill et al. (2010).

19. Stonehill et al. (2010).

20. Owen, I. (2010). Breaking the mold: Combining community schools with expanded learning time to help educationally disadvantaged students. Washington, DC: Center for American Progress.

21. See Blank et al. (2010).

REUBEN JACOBSON *is senior associate for research and strategy at the Coalition for Community Schools at the Institute for Educational Leadership.*

MARTIN J. BLANK *is president of the Institute for Educational Leadership and director of the Coalition for Community Schools.*

*LA's BEST reflects on how its values-based pro-
gram-delivery design positively affects youth
development.*

5

Expanded learning the LA's BEST way

Carla Sanger, Paul E. Heckman

AS FEDERAL AND STATE policymakers and many education researchers and experts suggest, expanding the learning day for students
makes sense. Given the demographic trends—women increasingly
entering the workforce and low-income families working multiple
jobs—children and youth need supervision and opportunities to
learn in the hours between 3:00 and 6:00 P.M. Although research
acknowledges the need for and the benefits of learning opportunities during the afternoon hours, the debate within education circles remains as to what constitutes the appropriate use of that time.
This chapter offers a reflection on how LA's BEST built its values-
based program-delivery model to support positive youth
development.

Common approaches in the field

In an educational climate that stresses tougher testing measures
and laments how far behind students from economically chal-
lenged neighborhoods lag, some educators define expanded

NEW DIRECTIONS FOR YOUTH DEVELOPMENT, NO. 131, FALL 2011 © WILEY PERIODICALS, INC.
Published online in Wiley Online Library (wileyonlinelibrary.com) • DOI: 10.1002/yd.409

learning to be strictly academic,[1] whereas others aim to retain enrichment components but miss the mark by failing to include community-based partnerships. These common approaches are predicated on the observation that students need more time on school skills and tasks than the regular school day offers them. But the more academics are emphasized, the less time there is for spontaneous conversation, probing interests, and sharing of experiences that fuel self-expression.

In today's rapidly evolving, unpredictable global society, children need to be able to think creatively, to solve problems, and to work cooperatively. Ideally, expanding the learning day is an opportunity to plan activities that are a natural outgrowth from children's needs and interests, what they care about, and what they wonder about. LA's BEST is a model designed to meet children's needs and interests.

The LA's BEST model

Established in 1988, LA's BEST After School Enrichment Program (LA's BEST) was created by Los Angeles Mayor Tom Bradley to address an alarming rise in the lack of adequate adult supervision and educational support of high-risk children during the critical hours between 3:00 and 6:00 P.M. Two massive bureaucracies, the City of Los Angeles and the Los Angeles Unified School District (LAUSD), agreed to cooperate with local communities through a 501(c)(3) nonprofit public benefit corporation.

Since inception, LA's BEST has grown from a pilot at ten elementary school sites to 180 sites (operating summer programs in 101 school sites), serving more than 28,000 low-income students every school day during the hours after school, at no cost to their parents. LA's BEST serves students in neighborhoods most plagued by gang violence and entrenched poverty. On average, 90.5 percent of the school population at LA's BEST sites qualifies for the federal subsidy for free or reduced lunch. Students at these sites are on average 49 percent female and 51 percent male; and 82

NEW DIRECTIONS FOR YOUTH DEVELOPMENT • DOI: 10.1002/yd

percent Hispanic, 9.3 percent African American, 5.7 percent Asian Pacific Islander and Filipino, and 3 percent Caucasian.

In addition to homework help, field trips, sports, and recreation, LA's BEST either creates the curriculum or adapts existing curricula from others (e.g., the Celebrate Science! Program adapted from a curriculum developed by scientists at NASA's Jet Propulsion Laboratory). Additionally, LA's BEST holds annual citywide weekend activities including the Celebrate Science! Fair, Community Jam Against Violence, Dance and Drill Team Showcase, BEST Fit Health Festival, and more than a dozen others. LA's BEST mobilizes and maintains a vast array of external networks, from families, schools, communities, private businesses, other national organizations, and government legislators. As a result, an abundance of resources is available and opportunities for students abound, far beyond the usual offerings of an after-school program.

LA's BEST is a sustainable, large-scale partnership that includes the city, the school district, and the private sector. Over the last two decades, more than $23 million has come from private individuals, corporations, and foundations to support this work to supplement more than $230 million from city, state, and federal government. Even under changing educational climates, LA's BEST remains true to its mission, focusing on engagement and the interests of students and consistently building relationships among adults, students, families, communities, and schools.

Our definition of expanded learning

Our definition and meaning for expanded learning builds on our experience at LA's BEST, as well as research in related fields. LA's BEST values learning that happens all day long in the many places that surround a child's development. The result is a massive set of memories and mental models that guide individuals during their daily lives in and out of school and throughout their lives. The expanded and dynamic process of gaining knowledge throughout a lifetime reflects our definition of expanded learning.

Our view challenges the exclusive emphasis on curriculum. Lauren Resnick, an educational psychologist, describes learning and the classroom processes involved in school knowledge in this way:

[It] encourage[s] the idea that the "game of school" is to learn symbolic rules of various kinds, that there is not supposed to be much continuity between what one knows outside school and what one learns in school. There is growing evidence, then, that not only may schooling not contribute in a direct and obvious way to performance outside school, but also that knowledge acquired outside school is not always used to support in-school learning. Schooling is coming to look increasingly isolated from the rest of what we do.[2]

School knowledge has a limited long-term payoff outside of school, but still determines the nature of the activities and learning that is valued inside classrooms. The result is that students' learning diminishes as activities in which they participate correspond to school-like activities.

Learning is happening and expanding outside of school every day.[3] Children are learning in their immediate environment.[4] Amanti, Gonzales, and Moll argue that what children learn inside and outside of school constitute "funds of knowledge."[5] All children possess funds of knowledge, and that knowledge should be equivalently valued.

The conditions for expanding learning opportunities

We now turn to the conditions that we have within the LA's BEST program to promote students' engagement and learning, expanding both the use of children's existing funds of knowledge and new learning. Establishing conditions in a program, rather than selecting and focusing on individuals' characteristics, has strong support in research.[6] However, the environment and the development of smartness require attention to student engagement.

High-wage and high-skill jobs usually are associated with more years of schooling. However, because the focus of today's education policy is on increasing test scores, educational attainment and the ability of the economically poorest students to gain the skills for these jobs has taken a back seat. Educational attainment is lacking in low-income neighborhoods across the country. Large numbers of economically poor adolescents are dropping out of school.[7] Without educational attainment, these students will not receive the benefits of more years of schooling, including higher incomes, greater civic participation, and improved physical health.[8] Instead, efforts are mounted to improve students' test scores and grades. These measures weakly predict how well students will do and how likely they are to succeed in their lives after precollegiate and postsecondary education.[9]

Educational attainment is more likely to increase as students' educational engagement increases. Paying attention to engagement is also significant because:

[T]he very act of being engaged also adds to the foundation of skills and dispositions that is essential to live a productive, satisfying life after college. That is, students who are involved in educationally productive activities in college are developing habits of mind and heart that enlarge their capacity for continuous learning and personal development.[10]

A National Academy volume, Engaging Schools, suggests features of programs that make these successes possible—cognitive, behavioral, and emotional engagement.[11] LA's BEST strives in each site program to provide children and youth with challenging tasks, encourage learning of valued skills, promote strong social relationships with adults and peers, and support positive identities.[12] A former LA's BEST student, who is now a student at the University of California, Los Angeles (UCLA), noted in response to a 2009 alumni survey: "LA's BEST did a great job allowing me, a kid that was full of energy and curiosity, to try many new things that I may not have otherwise. From sports to plays and field trips, I had some of the best times of my childhood while enrolled in LA's BEST."

A report by the National Research Council, Community Programs to Promote Youth Development, amplified important qualities of educational activities that will likely engage children and youth in their learning, such as active construction of knowledge; disciplined inquiry; relevance of material being studied to the student and his or her community culture; regular feedback on progress; opportunities to rethink work and understanding; recognition of and use of students' knowledge, interests, and dispositions; and students working together and tutoring each other.[13] Children and adults will be more likely to work together among themselves and with adults when their teachers care for them and hold them and their experiences and learning in high regard.[14]

At each LA's BEST site, the staff—the majority of whom are Latino or African American college students between the ages of 18 and 25 who live within two miles of the school site where they work—explicitly focus on developing the learning contexts at their particular site so that it positively influences children's learning in diverse cultural situations.[15] Attention is paid to activities and practices that encourage engagement and learning—homework support, educational enrichment, recreational enrichment, and a healthy snack.[16]

What sets LA's BEST apart from other programs is its values-based rather than rules-based approach to program delivery. For example, because one of the values LA's BEST espouses is that "nothing we do is as important as the effect it has on a child," each staff person has authority to change any plan or activity based on the responses of students engaged in that activity. Staff members are trained to observe students, probe for authentic responses, and modify activities or change plans accordingly. With a project-based learning approach used as a guideline, LA's BEST sites have the autonomy to structure individual programs as they deem appropriate to meet students' needs and interests. Together, these features engage the children in their learning and development.

Evidence of success

From its inception, LA's BEST board of directors set one goal for the organization as a whole—to encourage and determine in what ways LA's BEST made a positive difference in the life of a child. Annually, UCLA's Center for Research on Evaluation, Standards and Student Testing (CRESST) works with LA's BEST internal evaluation staff, administration, and field staff to discuss what indicators might show such a difference. A participatory evaluation evolves annually. Individual funders also request evaluations to see how successful LA's BEST has been in reaching specific goals set by their grants. These may include, but are not limited to, increased school-day attendance, increased prosocial behaviors, and more evidence of cooperative learning in the regular classroom.

Independent studies of the LA's BEST program show results of our efforts. CRESST conducted fourteen external evaluation studies of the program's effects. In A Decade of Results, CRESST examined student records, including test scores, regular school day attendance, language redesignation, and student retention. Their findings suggested that LA's BEST students compared to non-LA's BEST students in the same schools showed greater motivation and enthusiasm for school and greater trust of adults in their school environment.[17]

A 2005 study, Keeping Kids in School: An LA's BEST Example, found that LA's BEST students were 20 percent less likely to drop out of school. Denise Huang, the principal evaluator, disclosed that, "Teachers noted positive changes in social skills, classroom behavior, discipline and social interactions as a result of the program."[18] And LA's BEST parents reported they volunteered at school and participated in other school activities significantly more frequently than non–LA's BEST parents. In addition, LA's BEST parents had greater expectations for their children attaining higher education. These results occurred alongside of the continued enhancement of school attendance, even seven years after they left the program.

In 2006, CRESST conducted a qualitative study, with the use of a grounded-theory approach, to assess aspects of social capital within LA's BEST. Findings suggested that staff–student relationships in LA's BEST in terms of trust, support, and bonding are a good predictor of student engagement, student plans for continuing education, and student belief in future success.[19] Supportive and belonging relationships between adults and children involved in a program convey to students that they have the unconditional regard of adults and that the adults can be trusted to look out for their interests. For these relationships to develop, children and youth have to know that their interests influence what happens. In these ways, adults in the LA's BEST's program nurture students' development, their thinking, their interests, and their well-being.[20]

In 2006, James Catterall of UCLA investigated the nature and extent of learning in each of the respective art programs—music, drama, visual arts, and dance—in LA's BEST After School Arts Program (ASAP). Nearly 60,000 students participated in these ten-week ASAP artist-educator residencies. The study found that ASAP courses provided students with high-quality learning experiences that led to significant achievements in standards-based learning in the arts. Another CRESST longitudinal study commissioned by the U.S. Department of Justice in 2007 found that former students in LA's BEST were 30 percent less likely to be involved in crime over time, findings that crossed ethnicity, gender, and geography in the LA's BEST program.

These studies and other data analyses help our out-of-school program staff to examine and discuss relationships between existing empirical and theoretical research we learn from child, staff, family, and teacher surveys and anecdotes. For example, data from incident reports, attendance records, parent and student surveys, and independent evaluations are used in a number of ways, such as to suggest corrective actions at the site level, propose policy changes for addressing program issues, and identify needed staff development. Data from student surveys are used to assess student satisfaction with the program and help identify specific strengths and weaknesses of a program at each site. Traveling staff use data from the surveys to recommend changes in program activities, recommend staff development courses for specific staff members, and identify potential new topics of interest for the students. Finally, results from student surveys are used in grant proposals to secure additional funding for the program.

Student engagement not only influences outcomes within the LA's BEST program, but has an effect on advancing the important benefits of individuals graduating from high school, going on to college, and making positive contributions in their own lives and to society at large. LA's BEST is currently tracking alumnae to discover to what extent engagement in its programs led to different patterns of course selection in postsecondary education and jobs or careers later in life. We also would like to explore correlations between these later-in-life success patterns and attendance and participation patterns in LA's BEST, and norm-referenced test data and school grades, while these alumnae were in elementary school.

A comprehensive view of expanded learning

Today's policy debates about expanded learning tend to favor academic criteria over opportunities that promote conversations and explorations about student interests, engagement, and fun because of the increasing pressure for more direct instruction in skill-specific academics. Freedom to set conditions in after-school programs will not happen without political will, support, and financial resources to embrace the view that students are learning all the time. Educators need to pursue coordinated advocacy aimed at convincing decision makers that expanding the learning day is only as good as the conditions that encourage student engagement and do not rigidify after-school programs. And, we need to see to it that programs have sufficient funding to make the connections with our students and for students to make connections to each other, their schools, their families, their communities, and other cultures.

We encourage those who know how important student engagement is to have strength in their resolve to continue a practice that values the knowledge children are building every moment. We urge those who currently undervalue out-of-school-time programs to give them the full consideration they demonstratively deserve. That is the challenge and opportunity for the more comprehensive view of expanded learning such as modeled in LA's BEST.

Notes

1. Rocha, E. (2008). *Expanded learning time in action: Initiatives in high-poverty and high-minority schools and districts.* Washington, DC: Center for American Progress. Retrieved from http://www.americanprogress.org /issues/2008/07/elt_report1.html.

2. Resnick, L. (1987). The 1987 presidential address: Learning in and out of school. *Educational Researcher, 16*(9), 13–20.

3. Ginsburg, K. R. (2007, January). The importance of play in promoting healthy child development and maintaining strong parent-child bonds. *Pediatrics, 119*(1), 182–191.

4. Leander, K. M., Phillips, N. C., & Taylor, K. H. (2010). The changing social spaces of learning: Mapping new mobilities. *Review of Research in Education, 34,* 329–393.

5. González, N., Moll, L., & Amanti, C. (2005). *Funds of knowledge: Theorizing practices in households.* Mahwah, NJ: Lawrence Erlbaum.

6. Sternberg, R. J., & Grigorenko, E. L. (2006). Cultural intelligence and successful intelligence. *Group & Organization Management, 31*(1), 27–39.

7. Levin, H. M. (2009, January/February). The economic payoff to investing in educational justice. *Educational Researcher, 38*(1), 9; Miao, J., & Haney, W. (2004). High school graduation rates: Alternative methods and implications. *Educational Policy Analysis Archives, 12*(55), 42. Retrieved from http://epaa.asu.edu/epaa/v12n55/; Orfield, O., Losen, D., Wald, J., & Swanson, C. B. (2004). *Losing our future: How minority youth are being left behind by the graduation rate crisis.* Cambridge, MA: The Civil Rights Project at Harvard University, and Washington, DC: The Urban Institute. Retrieved from http://www.urban.org/uploadedPDF/410936_LosingOurFuture .pdf.

8. Levin, H. M. (1998). Educational performance standards and the economy. *Educational Researcher, 27*(4), 4–10; Levin, H. M. (1978, Winter). Educational performance standards: Image or substance? *Journal of Educational Measurement, 15*(4), 309–319.

9. Sternberg, R. J. (1997, October). The concept of intelligence and its role in lifelong learning and success. *American Psychologist, 52*(10), 1030–1037.

10. Kuh, G. D. (2003, March/April). Learning about engagement from NSSE. *Change, 25.*

11. National Research Council and the Institute of Medicine. (2004). *Engaging schools: Fostering high school students' motivation to learn.* Washington, DC: The National Academies Press, Committee on Increasing High School Students' Engagement and Motivation to Learn.

12. Eccles, J. S., Barber, B. L., Stone, M., & Hunt, J. (2003). Extracurricular activities and adolescent development. *Journal of Social Issues, 59*(4), 865–889.

13. National Research Council and Institute of Medicine. (2002). *Community programs to promote youth development.* Washington, DC: National Academy Press, Committee on Community-Level Programs for Youth.

14. Collins, A., Brown, J. S., & Newman, S. E. (1989). Cognitive apprenticeship: Teaching the craft of reading, writing, and mathematics. In L. B. Resnick (Ed.), *Knowing, learning, and instruction: Essays in honor of Robert Glaser* (pp. 453–494). Hillsdale, NJ: Lawrence Erlbaum.

15. Brown, J. S., Collins, A., & Duguid, P. (1989). Situated cognition and the culture of learning. Educational Researcher, *18*(1), 32–42.

16. Cole, M. (1996). *Cultural psychology: A once and future discipline.* Cambridge, MA: The Belknap Press of Harvard University Press.

17. Baker, E., Gibbons, B., Huang, D., Kim, K., & Lee, C. (2000). *A decade of results: The impact of the LA's BEST After School Enrichment Program on subsequent student achievement and performance.* Los Angeles, CA: Center for the Study of Evaluation (CSE), University of California, Los Angeles.

18. Huang, D., Kim, K., Marshall, A., & Pérez, P. (2005). *Keeping kids in school: An LA's BEST example.* Los Angeles, CA: National Center for Research on Evaluation, Standards and Student Testing (CRESST), University of California, Los Angeles.

19. Huang, D. (2006). *Exploring the intellectual, social and organizational capitals at LA's BEST.* Los Angeles, CA: National Center for Research on Evaluation, Standards, and Student Testing (CRESST), University of California, Los Angeles.

20. Commission on Children at Risk. (2003). *Hardwired to connect: The new scientific case for authoritative communities.* New York: Institute for American Values with the YMCA of the USA & Dartmouth Medical School.

CARLA SANGER *is the president and CEO of LA's BEST After School Enrichment Program.*

PAUL E. HECKMAN *is professor and the associate dean of UC Davis School of Education.*

The After-School Corporation developed the Expanded Learning Time (ELT/NYC) initiative out of the most effective elements of after-school programs, charter schools, and other expanded learning strategies.

6

The After-School Corporation's approach to expanded learning

Anne-Marie E. Hoxie, Lisa DeBellis, Saskia K. Traill

THE AFTER-SCHOOL CORPORATION (TASC) follows the national discussion on expanded learning initiatives with much interest. TASC believes that by increasing the amount of time that students spend in school, students can participate in diverse activities that go beyond the structured school curricula that characterize many of our schools nationwide. TASC's expanded learning strategy is to re-engineer schools to meet the range of student needs by adding more learning time to the school day, while supporting families, communities, and schools working collaboratively. This chapter lays out the research basis for TASC's approach to expanded learning time and opportunities (ELTO), a description of TASC's model and how it is being implemented in New York City, and a discussion of how TASC is measuring its success.

Research background

TASC brings together three main bodies of research around reform efforts that have been developed to respond to the needs

NEW DIRECTIONS FOR YOUTH DEVELOPMENT, NO. 131, FALL 2011 © WILEY PERIODICALS, INC.
Published online in Wiley Online Library (wileyonlinelibrary.com) • DOI: 10.1002/yd.410

and challenges of today's educational system. First, we draw on work based on the charter school movement and the related research. Second, we describe the main findings from the research on after-school programs. Lastly, we discuss expanded learning time initiatives that have been implemented in several cities in the country.

Charter schools have received a great amount of attention in recent years. One of the core features of successful charter school models is an increase in instructional time, a strategy designed to promote academic achievement.[1] A recent study including nearly all New York City's charter school students found that high-performing charter schools in New York City shared a set of common features, including giving students more time to learn, and especially more time to focus on English language arts.[2] Charter school students who attend schools with longer school days and years showed significant academic improvements. Students who attended a longer school day as part of The Knowledge Is Power Program (KIPP) charter school network significantly outperformed a comparison group in math and English language arts assessments in grades five through eight.[3]

Research on after-school programs also informs TASC's expanded learning model. Numerous studies show the positive impacts after-school programs have on children and youth.[4] Children and youth who are left unsupervised after school are at risk for engaging in drug use, acting out in aggressive ways, and demonstrating social withdrawal or depressive behaviors.[5] Participation in structured activities outside of school, on the other hand, is associated with decreased likelihood of criminal activity, positive social skill development and social behaviors, and building of self-confidence and self-esteem.[6] Research also shows that high-quality after-school programs help students to achieve more academically[7] and are associated with decreased likelihood of high school dropout.[8]

Evaluations of TASC's own after-school programs, developed in the late 1990s to offer school-based enrichment programs to hundreds of children per school, also show that programs improve student achievement and promote student growth as evidenced by standardized test score gains and improved school attendance rates.[9] The results of a large-scale, longitudinal evaluation, for example, demonstrated that participants in TASC-model programs had greater gains in their mathematics standardized scores than matched nonparticipants.[10] The researchers found that length of time enrolled in TASC programs and number of days attended were correlates of educational outcomes. Students who participated in TASC-model programming for at least two years and attended at least sixty days of programming per year experienced the greatest gains on mathematics standardized test scores. In addition, Black and Latino participants and students eligible for free lunch showed the greatest academic gains, providing evidence that TASC programs helped to close the achievement gap.[11]

The third body of research draws from the growing number of expanded learning initiatives across the country. Miami-Dade County Public Schools, for example, extended both the school day and year in thirty-nine schools as part of a school reform strategy known as the School Improvement Zone.[12] Students who attended "Zone" schools did not significantly outperform peers from comparison schools on reading and writing assessments.[13] A literature review from the past twenty-five years concluded that there is a clear difference between merely increasing time in school and increasing engaged time.[14] In short, positive impacts do not appear to result from more time, but effects emerge when more time is used well.

In 2005, Massachusetts launched an Expanded Learning Time initiative to expand the school day or year in selected schools. Typically, schools lengthened the school day by a total of 300 hours per year. The initiative's goal is to improve student outcomes in core subjects, expand opportunities for enrichment, and improve teacher instruction with greater planning time and professional development.[15] Implementation of the Massachusetts model thus far shows variation.[16] Likely because of this variation, a recent study reveals that although the initiative had a positive effect on fifth-grade students' standardized science assessment scores, researchers did not find effects on other outcomes, such as improving school attendance rates or increasing the amount of time students spent doing their homework.[17] This highlights the challenge in ensuring that initiatives are implemented as planned while also affording schools and community-based organizations the freedom to develop customized strategies and activities to improve student outcomes.

TASC's model

Building upon these bodies of research, TASC developed its ELTO model, ELT/NYC, in partnership with the New York City Department of Education and the Department of Youth and Community Development. TASC's ELT/NYC model is designed to scale throughout the public school system the opportunities typically afforded only to students whose families win a spot in a promising charter school through a lottery. The primary objective of TASC's ELT/NYC model is to improve students' chances for future success by increasing academic performance and more importantly, putting children on track to graduate from high school and be college ready. We aim to improve student performance on standardized tests, increase students' school attendance, and develop children's social skills and behavioral adjustment through a well-rounded combination of core academics, enrichments, and activities that meet educational needs while inspiring success. Ten schools began implementing the ELT/NYC model in 2008 as part of a pilot. In 2010, TASC added seven more schools.

In TASC's ELT/NYC model, schools work with community partners to expand the learning day to 6 P.M., so that a school day is re-engineered to include more time for core academics, individualized instruction, and hands-on learning experiences. Schools offer three more hours of time each day to allow students to develop a variety of skills through engaging learning opportunities. The ELT/NYC model is balanced to include academic support and enrichment activities, arts, sports and recreation, social development activities, and supper.

The model outlines a relative balance of activities, such that schools provide academic supports and enrichments for at least 40 percent of the expanded learning hours (for a fifteen-hour weekly schedule, this corresponds to a minimum of six hours per week). Arts, social development, fitness, and recreation together consist of at least 30 percent of a school's weekly expanded time, or a minimum of four and a half hours per week. To maximize time on task, schools spend no more than 25 percent of their weekly expanded hours offering a third nutritious meal in the day (supper or snack) and conducting dismissal, specifically no more than thirty minutes a day for supper and fifteen minutes a day for dismissal. At least 10 percent of a school's expanded time involves physical activity, or the equivalent of ninety minutes per week. At one elementary school (see Figure 6.1), a third-grade student experiences a seamless day at school from 8:00 A.M. until dismissal at 6:30 P.M. The student's day is infused with activities typically reserved for after-school programming. The school's community partner joins the school teaching staff in the morning and delivers instruction and activities in partnership with school day teachers.

TASC's model requires a meaningful partnership between schools and community partners. Teachers and other school staff meet with community partners for professional development and plan activities collaboratively. Where TASC's after-school programs were managed by community organizations, often independently from the schools in which they were housed, the cornerstone of the ELT/NYC model is the school-community partnership. This makes for two critical roles in ELT/NYC schools: the school's instructional leader and the community partner's full-time site coordinator. The instructional leader is a school staff member selected by the principal to ensure learning outcomes are met throughout the day. He or she ensures that there is ongoing communication and collaboration between the school day staff and the community partners, so that students have seamless transitions between teacher-led and community-educator-led activities.

NEW DIRECTIONS FOR YOUTH DEVELOPMENT • DOI: 10.1002/yd

Figure 6.1. A sample of a student's schedule at an ELT/NYC school

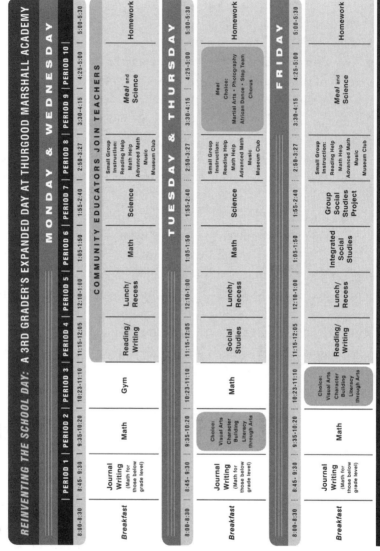

The full-time site coordinator, hired by the community partner, often with the principal's input, also plays a key role in this partnership. This person leads the community partner in its school collaboration. He or she works full-time on the initiative and integrates activities between the school and partner staff members.

Strong and effective collaboration between the school and the community partner is vital for the success of the model. In many cases, schools and community partners work for many years together, and in other cases, new partnerships form. Schools select organizations based on the partners' ability to help meet the school vision, partners' expertise, relationship to the community, and capacity to deliver relevant and engaging curriculum.

In TASC's ELT/NYC schools, activities are led by a combination of community partner educators, activity specialists, and certified teachers who work full-time in the school. Each school–community team determines the appropriate staffing. Certified teachers who stay for additional hours during the week are paid "per session," in accordance with their union contract. Some of the most successful strategies are those that partner community partner staff members with school-day teachers. It helps keep costs down, allows teachers the flexibility to teach topics in a way that they may not have time for during the typical school day, and gives students the chance to spend time with their teachers in a more relaxed environment.

One example of such a strong collaboration is at the Island School, P.S. 188, where the principal blends small-group instruction time by bringing teachers together with teaching artists from Educational Alliance, the school's community partner. Together, teachers and teaching artists deliver a rich social studies curriculum, bringing an additional hour for social studies to the school day and broadening students' opportunities for learning new material in interesting ways, such as writing plays related to a culture they are studying, preparing and eating foods from that culture, or creating art projects related to the curriculum. Strong collaboration is also evident at P.S. 636, where the school and community partner developed one coordinated behavioral modification strategy for the school so that students would have consistent rules throughout the day. In addition, the site supervisor for the community partner was part of the team that selected teacher hires for the school.

Ultimately, TASC's model is a whole-school initiative, but at this point in the pilot only some of the schools are able to serve nearly all of their students. There are challenges that some schools and some students face because of circumstances like school size and family needs. Students and parents who choose not to participate most often cite transportation as their main barrier to participation, because school transportation is not available at 6 P.M.

Building and sustaining TASC's ELT/NYC model

The launch of TASC's ELT/NYC model was not without its challenges. For years, community organizations fought to gain the leadership role they played in a school's after-school hours. Relinquishing this role to the school's principal felt like a loss of power and led to concerns from some organizations that after-school would turn into "more school" with no need for the "non-school activities." TASC's intermediary role helped to address these concerns. As part of the model, joint planning teams were developed between a school and its partner. Rather than focus on turf issues and access to various resources in the beginning, the joint planning sessions were designed so that schools and partners could gradually develop a shared vision for how to coordinate activities, budgets, and data sharing. Over time, concerns about budget sharing lessened, and solutions to common issues were developed and disseminated among partners. In fact, all community partners in the pilot group indicated that they would like to expand to another school.

However, despite the initial challenges, the model is sustainable for two core reasons. First, the model is designed to be cost-efficient. The addition cost is $1,600 per student per year, whereas the per-pupil cost for the traditional school day is $17,929.[18] In

Citizen Schools, a national nonprofit organization, shares lessons learned through years of experience developing and sustaining effective partnerships with schools around the country.

7

Citizen Schools' partner-dependent expanded learning model

Eric Schwarz, Emily McCann

IN 2005, THE CLARENCE EDWARDS middle school in Boston was failing. It was one of the lowest-performing schools in the city and on the verge of closure. Today, the school is thriving as one of Boston's highest-performing middle schools. Over the course of four years, the school eliminated the achievement gap for students in mathematics and erased 80 percent of the state gap on literacy and science standardized tests. In addition, family demand for the school in Boston's choice system[1] rose exponentially from a dismal seventeen to nearly five hundred families.

The catalyst for this dramatic turnaround was the implementation of a new, partner-dependent expanded learning time and opportunities model in September 2006, which extended the day by three hours and created partnerships with a few select community organizations to deliver instruction and programming during the expanded hours.

Citizen Schools, a nonprofit organization that has delivered after-school and expanded day programming at middle schools

NEW DIRECTIONS FOR YOUTH DEVELOPMENT, NO. 131, FALL 2011 © WILEY PERIODICALS, INC.
Published online in Wiley Online Library (wileyonlinelibrary.com) • DOI: 10.1002/yd.411

since 1995, signed on as the school's lead partner and has served the entire sixth grade during the afternoon hours since the fall of 2006. Citizen Schools focuses on the middle school years because middle school students are particularly in need of the kind of relevant learning, meaningful relationships, and rigorous studies that Citizen Schools' programming provides.[2] According to Dr. Carol R. Johnson, superintendent of the Boston Public Schools, "Our Edwards Middle School partnership with Citizen Schools has become a new model that shows the potential for how expanded learning time can truly transform teaching and learning at an underperforming school."

Some of the most successful charter and traditional schools across the country have named longer school days as a critical component of their success with students. In fact, in a 2009 survey administered by the National Center on Time & Learning, a vast majority of ELT schools (90 percent) ranked extended time as very important to meeting their educational goals.[3]

Expanded learning is becoming a central strategy of education reformers. As the concept gains momentum, the country has an opportunity that might come along once in a generation—an opportunity to change the way we structure the learning day dramatically.

Still, questions remain. Under what conditions is expanded learning most successful? What are the most effective staffing models of expanded learning that can support teachers and prevent teacher burnout? What are schools doing to ensure that the additional time is differentiated from but aligned with the traditional school day and yields results with students? How do we make expanded learning cost effective and scalable, and what policy changes can help make that a reality?

This chapter will examine how partnering with strong community organizations can help answer these questions. We will look at some of the successes and challenges schools face in partnering with expanded learning opportunities (ELOs). We know that schools that simply add more time without a shift in staff or approach yield few results. We also know that a strong and dynamic partnership between a school and community organization can create a new model of instruction that excites kids, empowers staff, and engages parents (and the broader community) to drive achievement in a lasting way.[4]

Community partners as a resource

Most schools, particularly those in low-income areas, lack the capacity and the networks to manage—and optimize—interaction with community members given limitations of time, infrastructure, and expertise. Community organizations can broker these relationships and have a multiplier effect for schools; they can engage, coordinate, and support the involvement of additional staff, parents, volunteers, and donors within a school. Citizen Schools, for example, has a model predicated on community involvement in education and attracts and leverages scores of volunteers who give hundreds of thousands of hours of their time to schools and students every year.

Partnerships, by nature, require deep commitment, flexibility, and perseverance to succeed, so school leaders must take care to select only the most effective, results-oriented organizations with whom to partner—organizations that have a compelling model, excellent track record, and dedicated talent.

Although many community partner organizations have contributed meaningfully to school culture and student opportunities and achievement, expanded learning partnerships can magnify this impact through a seamless connection between the traditional and expanded day. ELO partners like Citizen Schools that work with students on academics, help them make the connection between current school work and future careers, and connect with parents, have the added benefit of more time to do that meaningful work. In addition, such partnerships provide an opportunity for deeper alignment between the partner organization's approach and the school's needs and priorities.

Leveraging partnerships to their full potential

According to the 2010 report, Expanded Time, Enriching Experiences, by the Center for American Progress, "Several expanded learning time schools and their partners are pushing the envelope beyond what either side had imagined the role of an external organization in the life of a school could be."[5] The report outlines the various roles partner organizations are playing in schools, including the provision of academic instruction and enrichment, teacher professional development, student health services, family outreach, and even administrative support with governance, funding, and pedagogical practice.

More and more, schools are looking for partnerships that are deeply collaborative and provide services closely aligned with school needs. Expanded learning programs offer schools and their community-organization partners the platform to develop more strategic, reciprocal partnerships focused on student engagement and achievement. In Citizen Schools' experience, the most successful partnerships have three characteristics: additional academic instruction that is aligned with the curricula taught in the traditional school day; a fresh set of activities and approaches that foster student motivation and teach school navigational skills; and the ability to mobilize external resources to drive and support student learning.[6]

In several schools, community partners are providing a second shift of educators to teach and engage students in the expanded hours. This model, in which community organization staff members assume instructional duties in the additional hours, has proven an effective antidote to teacher burnout, which has plagued many charter and other ELT schools.[7]

This second-shift model requires deep coordination and alignment among school and community organization staff to ensure that instruction—and the entire student experience—is seamless throughout the longer school day. In the best partnerships, leaders from the school and community organization serve as thought partners on issues of instruction, culture, and staff development.

NEW DIRECTIONS FOR YOUTH DEVELOPMENT • DOI: 10.1002/yd

At ELT schools from Boston to Oakland, California, Citizen Schools' second-shift staff members are considered part of the school staff. The Citizen Schools "campus director," who leads the organization's work at each partner site, serves in a role similar to a vice principal or sixth-grade dean and is an active member of the school's leadership team, offering expertise and sharing best practices gleaned from Citizen Schools' partnerships across the country.

The most successful ELT schools have used the longer school day as a catalyst for innovation across the entire school day, searching for new models of engagement and instruction. For example, at Jane Long Middle School in Houston, science teachers are using the additional science time afforded by a new block schedule in the first six hours of the day to review critical lessons such as science vocabulary, but also to focus on more hands-on, project-based lessons that get kids excited about science—a hallmark of Citizen Schools' apprenticeship-style learning. Schools that successfully infuse the school day with the activities and approaches pioneered by their community partners often see exceptional results. Jane Long Middle School had seen plummeting enrollment in the years prior to lengthening the school day. In the school's first ELT year with more project-based learning by Citizen Schools and other teachers, enrollment was up by 12 percent and absenteeism was down 20 percent.

In 2006, Citizen Schools partnered with three out of ten Massachusetts schools that participated in the state's Expanded Learning Time pilot, including the Edwards Middle School described previously, as well as the Salemwood School in Malden and Umana Academy in Boston. Citizen Schools offers school partners small-group academics and hands-on programming, including project-based learning activities such as the organization's signature "apprenticeships" where volunteers teach ten-week courses on careers and professions. In addition, Citizen Schools' staff helps with family communication and engagement, including organizing family-friendly events and making biweekly phone calls.

NEW DIRECTIONS FOR YOUTH DEVELOPMENT • DOI: 10.1002/yd

According to a 2009 research brief by Policy Studies Associates on the implementation and performance of these three schools—Edwards, Umana, and Salemwood—the partnerships were effective. Examination of the schools' performance on state standardized tests found consistent evidence of improved student learning. After two years, student proficiency in English and mathematics improved more at Citizen Schools' partner schools than at other initiative schools or Massachusetts middle schools overall, indicating the strong potential for partner-dependent expanded learning to help improve achievement for students who are struggling academically.[8]

Increasing the effectiveness of partnerships

Developing and maintaining a successful partnership requires deep investment from both parties, particularly when student achievement is at stake. Partners must commit to a shared set of goals, engage in clear and consistent communication, and demonstrate flexibility as the landscape shifts. Citizen Schools has launched eleven partnerships nationwide and, through secondary research, has developed a set of best practices in developing and sustaining effective school partnerships. This is not an exhaustive list, but reflects the most critical components of an effective partnership.

Planning

Start a comprehensive planning process that engages school and community partner leadership as early as possible, to gather ideas and minimize resistance. Partners should spend between six and twelve months gathering input from key constituents, including teachers, administrators, students, and families, and developing a model for increased learning time that aligns with the school's overall goals for student achievement. For Citizen Schools' national ELT pilot, each partner school appointed an ELT liaison.

Key elements of planning include agreement on school operations, including school-day structure, transportation, professional development alignment, union involvement, sharing of student performance data, joint training, and considerations for special needs students; academic alignment that extends the opportunity for students to practice and internalize state learning standards; and a communication plan for the whole school community.

Leadership

Leaders should participate actively in the planning and implementation phases and lead the communication plan. Citizen Schools assigns a leader at each school partner—the campus director—who oversees operations and instruction to ensure optimal partnership with the traditional school day. Ideally, the campus director works closely with the school principal and leading faculty to shape the partnership and make key decisions at the school level. Campus directors are typically former teachers from a traditional school setting or at Citizen Schools, and some of them are on a pathway to becoming school principals or taking other school leadership positions.

Expectations

It is essential that school and community partners are clear on expectations around specific roles and program delivery before programming commences. School leaders should understand their partner organization's program model thoroughly. Whenever possible, potential partners should arrange site visits to see schools and programs in action.

Expectations should be set early and codified in legal documents, including Memoranda of Agreement (MOAs) and school partnership agreements. MOAs generally capture details often discussed at the district level, including funding and data sharing. School partnership agreements address school-level details such as space, scheduling, and school operations. Partners may need to revisit agreements and manage expectations throughout the school year. These documents should highlight both nonnegotiable priorities and areas of flexibility.

A lack of clear expectations can lead to confusion for staff and students. For example, if all school administration and staff do not fully understand the transition to a mandatory longer day, there may be a lack of consistency in communication with students. In some instances, Citizen Schools has found it necessary to do follow-up communications and work on outlining consequences for students who leave school early even after the school year has begun. It is preferable, of course, for all staff to understand from the start that longer days are nonnegotiable for students.

Conversion vs. new site

When a community partner is transitioning its role in a school from an after-school provider to an ELO partner, it must work diligently to shift the perceptions of school leaders, faculty, and parents. This will help ensure alignment on roles, expectations, and program delivery.

Students, staff, families, and others should receive proper communications and education about the evolving role of the community partner. Communications might include a family orientation night and regular calls home to family. Partner organizations should also participate and present as part of school day meetings and orientations with teachers, student support staff, and the school's instructional leadership team.

Sharing data and measuring success

Quantitative measurements are required to assess the impact of the partnership on student achievement. In an expanded learning partnership, the school and community partner are accountable to a set of shared academic goals and student outcomes. Partners should work together to identify specific measures for evaluating the impact of the partnership and must be willing to collect and share as much data as possible to track results on an ongoing basis.

Partnership agreements should clearly outline expectations around shared data. In its partnership-expectations document,

Citizen Schools outlines that schools and districts must provide the organization access to student performance data, including short-cycle assessments, and that Citizen Schools' staff participate in instructional and leadership meetings in which performance data are discussed. In addition, Citizen Schools staff share data with regular-day teachers, both performance data from assessments offered in the extended day lessons, and observations from conversations with parents that Citizen Schools staff regularly conduct.

The balancing act

Successful partnerships usually require both schools and community partners to alter some of the ways they traditionally operate. Community organizations need to factor in school goals and needs while balancing academic, enrichment, and youth development demands. Schools may need to adapt to new approaches and styles practiced by partner staff.

Tensions over sharing space, behavior management styles, or teaching approaches may surface. The best way to alleviate these tensions is to develop solutions that bridge the gap collectively. Partnerships thrive when schools and partners are willing to think creatively and compromise when necessary, while staying focused on shared outcome goals and a vision of dramatically improved student achievement. For example, Citizen Schools has worked closely with one school principal to address her concerns about her students' relative dearth of physical activity. Together, the school and Citizen Schools rearranged the after-school sports schedule to take place at the conclusion of the Citizen Schools (so students could participate in both) and to develop more sports apprenticeships during Citizen Schools hours.

Citizen Schools had to demonstrate flexibility with a number of its partner schools, making tweaks to the organization's program model to accommodate schools' specific areas of focus. In order to ensure consistency in its implementation across its network of sites, Citizen Schools has developed a framework and program model with specific optional and mandatory features to allow for a certain level of flexibility while maintaining overall program quality and consistency.

During the initial planning stages, Citizen Schools' staff works with school leadership to determine how Citizen Schools' programming will help support the school's goals for student achievement. For instance, each school chooses a mathematics or English language arts focus for Citizen Schools' academic support block hours. Citizen Schools then hones its core program model to align with the schools' focus while maintaining the signature elements of the Citizen Schools model, including three hours of project-based "apprenticeship" learning weekly and at least five hours of academic practice, including structured homework time and academic lessons aligned with school needs.

Both schools and community partners may have a certain set of core principles that are nonnegotiable. It is best for those principles to be outlined as early as possible in the partner-selection process. Citizen Schools develops a set of principles for effective school partnerships that the organization uses to screen new school partnerships and to assess existing ones. Conditions and indicators for success include strong principal leadership, a culture of achievement and belief in student success, willingness to share data on student learning, and district commitment to reform. Although these conditions may rule out some schools, the ELT schools that partner with Citizen Schools are typically among the lowest-performing schools in their districts and states, with student poverty rates of 90 percent or more, and low rates of academic proficiency.

At Elmhurst Community Prep in Oakland, CA, the combination of strong leadership and a core belief in and commitment to students proved to be critical to a very successful first year. The school's principal, Laura Robell, ensured that the implementation of a partnership with Citizen Schools gets consistent support at all levels. Robell rallied teachers, administrators, Citizen Schools' staff, and all other school staff toward a common goal of providing an excellent learning experience for all students, all day. In addition, the Oakland School district provided significant support at

Elmhurst through a federal School Improvement Grant, for which the school qualified because of its persistent low performance.

Funding expanded learning in schools

In a time of contracting budgets, many schools and school districts are wondering how they can implement expanded learning in a cost-effective and scalable way. Although we believe a strong case can be made for new investments in high-quality ELT schools, given the country's fiscal challenges, the most viable funding mechanism in the short term is the reallocation of existing school funding sources to support ELTO in recognition of its unique ability to drive results and meet student and family needs.[9]

Based on our experience and research, there appear to be three primary levers districts and schools can use to direct more resources: changes in policy, changes in operations, and higher in-district student retention.

Policy and operations. Districts can garner more funds for expanded learning if constituents—led by parents, community organizations, and their champions—can influence policymakers to designate existing funding streams as viable sources of funds.

Some innovative schools are leading the way on developing cost-effective funding models that also drive results. These schools have reallocated resources within their control to fund a nine-hour day for the same amount of money other schools use to run much shorter schedules. The most promising of these strategies include:

- A modest increase in student to teacher ratios, an initiative that has had no adverse effect, in isolation, on student achievement
- The utilization of technology-based, individualized learning to complement traditional teacher-led instruction
- The employment of paraprofessionals during the traditional school day
- Coverage of one to two hours per week of regular class time by second-shift educators to allow professional development for

teachers to be offered during regular contracted hours, not on weekends or evenings when overtime pay is required.

Rocketship Education, a highly successful charter school network in San Jose, California, uses a unique hybrid education model where core teaching staff are supplemented by "Learning Lab" time, with computer-driven and tutor-driven instruction, that lengthens the school day by 100 minutes each day without additional teacher work time.

Finally, many school finance experts believe that operational savings in the central office, transportation, utility, or other non-academic budget line items could free up significant money to pay for expanded learning in schools.

Student retention

Schools can use expanded learning as a mechanism to retain students in the public school system. When schools and districts retain students through better offerings they also retain per-pupil allocations from the state and federal government, money they would have lost if students left the system. Over time, if expanded learning reduces dropout rates (as it has with Citizen Schools' participants) this will also increase enrollment and revenue for schools.

After partnering with Citizen Schools, Jane Long Middle School increased enrollment by 20 percent in its first year with an expanded time schedule, reversing a multiyear slide in enrollment. This increased enrollment more than paid for the bus the school required to send more children home at a later time. In addition, the school's principal chose to commit a significant portion of the school's Title I funds to pay for expanded learning, which allowed her to double the amount of science and social studies instruction that she provided sixth grade students in the regular school day hours.[10]

Schools and partners need to work closely to understand total expenses for expanded learning and identify committed sources of public and private revenue early. Citizen Schools has secured 60 percent of the required funding for direct program operations from public-sector sources and 40 percent through private-sector grants. Public-sector sources include district appropriations, Title I allocations, school improvement grants, and money set aside for state expanded learning initiatives. Private-sector support comes from foundations, corporations, and individual donors.

A solution for struggling schools

The best ELTO partnerships not only deliver an additional three hours of instruction at the end of the day, but also help schools reimagine and improve the first six hours, serving as a serious solution for chronically failing schools. Community partners, through well-designed curricula and fresh learning approaches, can engage, inspire, and support students in ways that breed confidence and resilience through the entire school day. In addition, partners' staff can serve as thought partners and colleagues to administrators and teachers and as community organizers, engaging parents and the larger community in driving student achievement. In turn, community organizations get the opportunity to be true school partners, integrated within a school and able to reach all students in a way that is nearly impossible as a traditional out-of-school-time program. This type of partnership requires community organizations to shift toward a more collaborative and likely more rigorous academic model that can challenge cultural norms. Organizations need to manage this thoughtfully.

Existing partnerships can serve as a model for schools looking to expand and redesign the school day to increase student achievement. We know, through experience and research, that the most critical inputs for strong, successful partnership include strong partner selection, diligent planning, ongoing communication and collaboration, and impact measurement. As new partnerships in this sector develop, we must track progress and share best practices. Ultimately, the partner-dependent model has the potential to drive significant achievement gains for students and help failing schools design a new school day that dramatically improves student achievement.

Notes

1. Boston Public Schools offers families a list of schools to which they can apply.

2. Balfanz, R. (2009). *Putting middle school grades students on the graduation path*. Westerville, OH: National Middle School Association.

3. Farbman, D. A. (2009). *Tracking an emerging movement: A report on expanded-time schools in America*. Boston: National Center on Time & Learning. Retrieved from http://www.timeandlearning.org/databasefullreport2009.html.

4. Traphagen, K., & Johnson-Staub, C. (2010). *Expanded time, enriching experiences: Expanded learning time schools and community organization partnerships*. Washington, DC: Center for American Progress. Retrieved from http://www.americanprogress.org/issues/2010/02/expanded_time.html; Massachusetts 2020. (2010). *More time for learning: Promising practices and lessons learned*. Boston: Author; Massachusetts 2020. (2010). *The Clarence Edwards Middle School: Success through transformation*. Boston, MA: Author. Retrieved from http://www.mass2020.org/files/file/Edwards%20Case%20Study%20FINAL.pdf.

5. Traphagen & Johnson-Staub. (2010).

6. Kolbe, T., Partridge, M., & O'Reilly, F. (2011*). Time and learning in schools: A national profile*. Boston, MA: National Center on Time & Learning.

7. Stuit, D. A., & Smith, T. M. (2009). *Teacher turnover in charter schools*. Nashville, TN: Vanderbilt University. Retrieved from http://www.ncspe.org/publications_files/OP183.pdf.

8. Woods, Y. M., & Reisner, E. R. (2009). *Citizen Schools' contribution to improved learning in expanded learning time schools*. Washington, DC: Policy Studies Associates.

9. Cunningham, K., Ojukwu, R., & Pinchback, J. (2011). *Extended learning time in public schools: Analysis of Citizen Schools cost, comparative benchmarks, overview of sustainable funding opportunities, and implications for Citizen Schools*. Boston: Bain & Company.

10. The Jane Long Middle School principal chose to lengthen the school day for all sixth graders in order to prepare students academically during their first year at the school and get them excited about middle school. Citizen Schools offers ELT programs targeted for seventh and eighth graders as well. School partners choose which model works for them based on local resources and needs.

ERIC SCHWARZ *is the CEO and a cofounder of Citizen Schools.*

EMILY MCCANN *is the president of Citizen Schools.*

Four principals from New York City, Los Angeles, and Houston share their schools' journeys of how they expanded learning time and opportunities to best meet their students' academic and developmental needs.

8

Building an expanded learning time and opportunities school: Principals' perspectives

Helen Janc Malone

EXPANDED LEARNING TIME and opportunities (ELTO) requires a committed school leader who is willing to partner with community-based organizations in order to provide strong academic and enrichment daily experiences for his or her students. This chapter examines four such leaders and the diverse approaches they took to implement ELTO in their schools.

Leo Politi Elementary School (Los Angeles), Jane Long Middle School (Houston), The Bronx School of Science Inquiry and Investigation (Bronx, New York), and Edward Bleeker Junior High School (Queens, New York) are among a growing number of public schools that are expanding their school hours and learning opportunities to serve their students better.[1] Located in resource-poor communities serving primarily low-income and minority children, the principals of these four schools transformed their

NEW DIRECTIONS FOR YOUTH DEVELOPMENT, NO. 131, FALL 2011 © WILEY PERIODICALS, INC.
Published online in Wiley Online Library (wileyonlinelibrary.com) • DOI: 10.1002/yd.412

buildings into full-day facilities that offer rigorous academic, enrichment, and developmental experiences in order to help their students overcome adversity and get ready for the next transition in their lives.

The impetus for the four veteran principals—Bradley Rumble (Leo Politi), Diana De La Rosa (Jane Long), Serapha Cruz (The Bronx School), and Valerie Sawinski (Edward Bleeker)—is a desire to help their students access quality education often available only in the top charter and private schools.[2] Principal De La Rosa explains: "We are surrounded by successful charter schools. So what happens if students don't win the lottery and can't attend a charter? Why should they receive poor education?... They deserve the same opportunities charters give, so that is the school's focus." Principal Sawinski agrees: "My goal was to offer activities that you would find in a prep school, where parents would be paying a lot of money for these activities. This levels the playing field for my children."

Another reason for ELTO is equity of opportunity for enrichment and positive adolescent development, opportunity generally unavailable in these resource-poor communities. Principal Cruz describes her school's neighborhood:

There aren't community resources offered right around here. It is not necessarily the case that the parents would be able to take them to different things on weekends or after school, so we really have to be that community resource hub where we can offer them all these things that they care about and enjoy and make them feel positive about school.

Principal De La Rosa shares a similar view:

We don't have parents that are sitting at home and waiting for the kids at 3 o'clock. We don't have kids who have had a model of schooling K–5. . . . We have multitude of languages and social ills that are affecting families, so we have to step up to the plate and say: "What is our role?" We have to do a lot more than a traditional school will have to do. For me, the school is here to meet the needs of the community, and you have to mold yourself to fill those needs.

NEW DIRECTIONS FOR YOUTH DEVELOPMENT • DOI: 10.1002/yd

Given a lack of opportunities in these communities, these princi-pals knew that their schools had to look different than the tradi-tional public schools. Principal De La Rosa continues: "The big one for me is to think outside the box. . . . We have to not just do the cookie-cutter model we have been doing forever and ever. Cookie-cutter wasn't cutting it here!"

To create a successful school experience that offers students quality academic, enrichment, and developmental opportunities, these four schools focused on five core elements—time, teacher buy-in, community partnerships, developmental services for stu-dents, and family involvement.

Creating an engaging schedule

The decision to expand learning time was guided by the individual school's circumstances. The Bronx School already had an extended time schedule when Principal Cruz took the helm; however, the schedule was strictly focused on the basics, which Principal Cruz felt was insufficient to support her students. The school thus invited community-based partners offering expanded learning opportunities (ELOs) to participate in a longer day. Leo Politi also had an expanded structure in place when Principal Rumble arrived. He continued to nurture the partnership with a citywide after-school program, LA's BEST, and, at the same time, built additional partnerships with community organizations.

For principals De La Rosa and Sawinski, the push came from the families and community members. Principal De La Rosa expanded the school schedule at the request of some fifty parents. At first, the school engaged teachers in the extended schedule, but experiencing teacher burn-out, the school reached out to quality ELOs, a strategy overwhelmingly supported by teachers, families, and students. Principal Sawinski also listened to her constituency and worked for over a decade to build community partnerships, transforming Edward Bleeker into a full-day, full-service commu-nity school. Together, all four principals recognized that their

NEW DIRECTIONS FOR YOUTH DEVELOPMENT • DOI: 10.1002/yd

students needed supports, structures, and opportunities beyond the academic core. The result was a longer school day with both academics and enrichment.

However, expanding time is only half of the equation. The other element is enrichment. Leo Politi starts the day with a before-school "Beyond the Bell Ready Set Go" program that engages children in computer time, arts, and reading. At seven, children are served breakfast, and the school day starts right before eight o'clock. Due to the school's partnership with LA's BEST, some students stay in school until after five o'clock and participate in a variety of LA's BEST extracurricular activities, as well as get involved in the Yard Habitat Project, an "urban oasis" outdoor classroom project run by the school created to help children learn about urban wildlife and biodiversity on the school grounds. Principal Rumble personally runs bird-watching tours for students, helping them learn about their environment.

Jane Long and The Bronx School both partner with a national ELO, Citizen Schools, but their schedules look different. Jane Long starts each day with 45-minute sports or club activities to get children motivated to engage in the four ninety-minute blocks of reading, mathematics, science, and social studies that follow. The Bronx School, on the other hand, offers hour-long periods of both the academic core and electives, including a before-school "zero period" dedicated to English language learners and a reading intervention for struggling readers. Both schools provide their sixth graders with the Citizen Schools experience, wherein students spend early afternoons doing homework, receiving tutoring assistance, and participating in the ten-week apprenticeships. The upperclassmen in these schools end their day after seven hours of class time. They then have an opportunity to participate in voluntary extracurricular activities primarily run by the school-day teachers.

Finally, the Edward Bleeker school offers eleven equal periods alongside test preparation, remediation support, and diverse extracurricular activities—band, drama, science Olympiad, flag football, community service—in partnership with health and family services agency, the Child Center of New York. Its sixth and seventh graders share the same academic and fine arts courses, while the eighth graders focus on the academics and foreign languages (instead of the fine arts). The flexibility to design a school schedule that best suits each grade level helps students access developmentally appropriate learning experiences tailored to support their academic and personal growth.

Focusing on teacher buy-in

Investing in teachers is the second critical component. Principal Rumble values his teachers, listens to their needs, and is a strong believer in collaboration through joint lesson planning and partnership building. Principal Cruz also invests in improving instruction, and encourages teacher professional development and collaboration through professional learning communities and shared decision making. She explains:

My thing was that if we can retain teachers and given them quality professional development, students should be able to get the academics that they need during the school day, and there should be a really small percentage, maybe five percent, that need additional academic help beyond what they are getting in the high-quality instruction during the day.

Quality instruction leaves students open to engage in enrichment and developmental opportunities beyond the core.

To keep her students motivated in a longer school day, Principal Cruz works with teachers to develop a "club culture," an expectation that all students, particularly seventh and eighth graders not involved in the Citizen Schools program, would participate in different clubs. To create this club culture, Principal Cruz talks with teachers from their first job interview to communicate an expectation that teachers should run clubs (teachers select the school year period and the contours of a club) and work with students outside the traditional hours on experiential learning. To ensure students take advantage of the many clubs offered at the school, the school runs "club fairs" in the fall, winter, and summer, and encourages students to select one activity for each semester.

Edward Bleeker offers a similar experience. Principal Sawinski's teachers are taking the initiative to create and run after-school programs.

For example, a mathematics teacher runs the "Best Buddies" program where students partner with a school serving autistic children, and the two groups develop peer relationships through joint activities and weekly communications. About 15 percent of Edward Bleeker teachers are involved in after-school programming, with the number and hours negotiated in the collective bargaining agreement.

However, it is not only the teacher-run after-school programs that help to build a positive teacher culture. Principal De La Rosa credits the work of Citizen Schools in motivating her teachers to improve their own practices inside the classroom. According to De La Rosa, when her teachers saw how motivated and engaged students were during the Citizen Schools hours, they felt encouraged to transform their own instructional practices and work with students on project-based learning and teamwork.

Building community partnerships

The third element principals added were community partners. Be it LA's BEST, Citizen Schools, or the Child Center of New York, each school has at least one major ELO partner that works on the school grounds in order to support students' academic and skill-building goals. One of the primary reasons for the partnerships is a recognition on the part of the principals that students need support beyond the traditional day and that ELOs offer expertise that benefit children and youth both academically and developmentally. Principal Rumble explains:

You can't do it alone. So, when a group like LA's BEST comes to the school and brings to the school structure and opportunities for students to engage in art and science activities in a way that is rigorous and engaging, they are making my job a lot easier, and I need to value them.

The partner selection varies by school. Leo Politi partnered with LA's BEST prior to Principal Rumble's tenure. Principal Sawinski partnered with the Child Center after applying for a grant. She gained additional ELOs after becoming a part of The After-School Corporation's (TASC) demonstration site for ELT/NYC. And, principals Cruz's and De La Rosa's school partnerships resulted from a competitive citywide selection process by Citizen Schools.

Both principals Cruz and De La Rosa applied to be Citizen Schools sites because of the organization's reputation as a high-quality program that helps urban children succeed academically. Citizen Schools works with sixth graders and assists with their academic and personal development. Citizen Schools is also favored because of the robust support structure it brings to each partner school. The organization supplies qualified staff who actively engage inside the classrooms, assisting teachers during the day and on the field trips, and serving as second-shift teachers during the afternoon hours. Citizen Schools' campus directors, also assigned to each partner school, work with principals to coordinate the program, apprenticeships, and the staff–school logistics. Principal De La Rosa says the Citizen Schools program adds value to her students' experiences:

[Citizen Schools] is changing the culture of the community. It helps kids build twenty-first century skills. There is opportunity for collaboration. There is an opportunity [for a student] to say: "I heard that from my teacher, but it still doesn't make sense, so can you present it in a different way?"

ELOs support school staff and above all, support students. And although issues of turf, funding, content delivery, and data access might initially arise, principal leadership and focus on collaboration help to alleviate the common partner issues. Principal Sawinski illustrates this point:

My teachers see it as benefiting "our children." Because it is our children, it is our building. It is not a matter of "my classroom, my resources." I provide my teachers with everything they need. . . Anything we have in this building is for the children, and that is how my teachers see it, so it wouldn't be "you are using my materials." Materials will be used, and they will be replaced!

Supporting student development

The fourth element is developmental services. Principal Rumble elucidates:

The most important thing is that we are not just producing test-takers. Our charge is to produce the whole child... It is really important not to lose sight of what you are trying to do by creating the whole child, so when the child matriculates to sixth grade, the academics are there, but there is also a depth of knowledge in many different fields, including social relationships.

Through extracurricular activities and the habitat project, Leo Politi students are not only learning about their community, but they are also actively engaging within it, building social relationships, and learning the value of community service and giving back.

The whole-child focus of the four schools also translates into support for individual student's mental and physical health. For example, Jane Long partners with the Memorial Hermann Healthcare Clinic to provide students with medical services. Additionally, to support students' social–emotional needs, a full-time social worker from the Memorial Clinic trains at the school, along with several interns. The school also offers peer mentoring and encourages students to problem solve on their own.

The Edward Bleeker school includes similar programs—grade-level counselors who move up with students for three years, building trusting student relationships that help adolescents prepare for high school. The school also runs peer mediation and has a full-time social worker hired through the New York State Mental Health Initiative. Additionally, the school recently received a grant for "Project 25," which provides the school with a substance-abuse specialist who works directly with students and their families. Access to personalized services beyond learning helps students get classroom ready and assists students in their personal development. Students additionally feel that the school staff cares about and for them, which increases student attendance and participation in school.

Involving families

The final component is an investment by the principals in family involvement. Before Jane Long expanded hours, students were dismissed from school by the early afternoon, leaving them to an unstructured, unsupervised environment. Today, their parents are able to pick them up. Principal De La Rosa describes the change:

When the day ended at 3 P.M., we had these masses of kids walking out in the community while parents were still at work. And, because of the socio-economics and the demographics of the community, there wasn't a parent at home or an alternative in the community. It was "give a kid a key and let them come home." Now, the kids are at school until 5:30 P.M. . . . . Now, basically, we have a traffic jam in front of the school because the parents can come by. . . . There are more kids going to a supervised home. Also, parents are saying: "Wow, the school is doing this for me. . . ." Our parent involvement in school activity is incredible. It has tripled since we had a traditional school day.

In addition to the more convenient hours of operation, Principal De La Rosa has invested in family involvement activities. For example, she runs workshops for parents to review how apprenticeships work, and how parents can access an on-line grading system and support student learning at home. The principal also holds monthly forums where family members come and discuss school policies, suggest improvement ideas, and volunteer to assist with diverse on-site opportunities.

Principal Sawinski finds that the longer school day is a great selling point for families. Families now not only want their children to attend Edward Bleeker School, but they are also more likely to be intimately involved with the school knowing what the school is doing to support their children—helping students with the academics, homework completion, tutoring, after-school activities, apprenticeships, high school and college readiness, and health and social services.

Principal Rumble uses his post as an opportunity to engage families in the school. He hosts monthly gatherings with parents— "coffee with the principal"—as well as Monday morning assemblies—short ceremonies where he honors students, motivates teachers, and communicates with families. These activities lead to family involvement.

Improving students' experiences

ELTO as a strategy offers schools flexibility to design schedules and provide supports and services based on the students' needs and local contexts. Principals are utilizing teachers to teach electives and/or run before- and after-school programs in addition to the traditional instructional hours. Principals are also reaching out to quality community-based organizations and agencies and creating in-school ELO partnerships whereby the partners serve to support academic goals and to offer personalized experiential and developmental services that address each individual student's needs. Finally, the principals are building relationships with families in order to encourage family involvement in school and at home.

Redesigning the school day is yielding positive student results. The four schools are seeing increases in students' grades, test scores, classroom participation, and attendance. As Principal Cruz suggests: "[Expanding the learning day] set a tone from the very beginning, a tone of high expectations. 'We expect you to be working hard, completing all of your homework, and be graduating from high school and college, and going into these different career fields'." At The Bronx School, the change is creating a sense of pride in students. Principal Cruz reflects: "When we first opened the school, the students could have cared less what school they went to . . . and now, we have really a culture of pride in school. Students are happy that they go to this school."

As these schools continue to implement their ELTO strategies, they all face a common challenge—wider student access. Although attendance is mandatory for students participating in Citizen Schools or school-day electives, access to such enrichment activities remains restricted to a portion of the school population because of budgetary, staffing, and/or resource constraints. At Leo Politi, for example, 30 percent of the students are engaged with LA's BEST. At Jane Long, less than a quarter of seventh and eighth graders are enrolled in the Citizen Schools program. This is a reality that all four principals would like to see changed, and they hope they can scale up their ELO efforts across grade levels in order to provide such opportunities to all their students.

Notes

1. For more information on the featured schools, visit: Leo Politi at http://wwww.lausd.k12.ca.us/Leo_Politi_EL/Home.html; Jane Long at http://ms.houstonisd.org/LongMS/; The Bronx School at http://www.ms331.org; and Edward Bleeker at http://www.jhs185.org.

2. Data collected for this article come from the following four interviews: Serapha R. Cruz, personal communication, November 12, 2010; Diana De La Rosa, personal communication, November 12, 2010; Bradley Rumble, personal communication, November 12, 2010; and Valerie Sawinski, personal communication, November 15, 2010.

HELEN JANC MALONE *is an advanced doctoral candidate at the Harvard Graduate School of Education focusing on youth development and education policy research.*

This concluding chapter examines the emerging themes, challenges, opportunities, and next steps for ELTO.

9

Next steps in the expanded learning discourse

Helen Janc Malone, Gil G. Noam

THE ACCOUNTABILITY MOVEMENT within K–12 education has prioritized school reform efforts that close the achievement gap. Both government and philanthropic sectors have made significant investments over the last decade toward innovative efforts that stand to boost student academic performance in low-performing schools.[1] Although the majority of the education reform attention has been paid to in-school classroom instruction, teacher quality, and principal and district leadership, there is a parallel, emerging movement to cultivate ideas that support closing of the opportunity gap—providing low-income children and youth in resource-poor communities with expanded learning that offers them a balance of academics, enrichment, and positive developmental experiences.

Expanded learning time and opportunities (ELTO) has emerged in recent years as a viable whole-school and whole-child strategy that both honors academic goals and supports broader educational and developmental ones. More schools serving low-income students are extending their schedules, using time as an important lever to expand learning opportunities. Although each expanded

NEW DIRECTIONS FOR YOUTH DEVELOPMENT, NO. 131, FALL 2011 © WILEY PERIODICALS, INC.
Published online in Wiley Online Library (wileyonlinelibrary.com) • DOI: 10.1002/yd.413

learning time school (ELT) customizes its schedule to fit the needs of its students, many schools are turning to community-based organizations that offer expanded learning opportunities (ELOs) as equal partners in a re-envisioned school day.

As expanded learning receives increased visibility, it is essential to clarify at the end of this volume a distinction that is often overlooked–many extended day supporters are primarily interested in more "time on task," making the existing traditional school day longer and dedicated solely to core academics, a focus different from the expanded day strategies. While alignment with extended efforts could be politically expedient, "more of the same" undermines the entire mission of a positive reform effort. Thus, it is paramount to stress the importance of preserving and supporting positive youth development programs and services offered by ELOs as a critical piece to expanded learning efforts such as the ELTO strategy.

The purpose of this issue is to examine a blended construct, ELTO, addressing the centrality of school–community partnerships as a viable expanded learning strategy to support broader student learning and positive developmental outcomes. The robust discussions provided in this issue highlight burgeoning research, promising policies, and a spectrum of effective practices that make the case for meaningful partnerships between ELTs and ELOs. This concluding chapter examines crosscutting themes, core challenges, and opportunities facing ELTO partnerships, and closes with concrete macrolevel steps the education field should consider within the expanded learning discourse.

Emerging themes

There are four core crosscutting themes that exemplify ELTO— focus on equity, quality use of time, relationship building, and commitment to data.

NEW DIRECTIONS FOR YOUTH DEVELOPMENT • DOI: 10.1002/yd

Focus on equity

It is important to recognize that equity issues are not only about academic achievement. Educators and youth development professionals alike recognize that high-poverty students benefit from diverse learning experiences beyond quality in-school instruction.[2] Children in privileged settings have more opportunities to explore nature and to engage in sports and arts. They also have better programming for an enriching summer and travel more with their families. All of these experiences represent forms of learning, physical activity, and the cultivation of the young mind. An ELTO approach tries to equalize some of these opportunities for high-poverty students. It would be highly problematic if the previously free time for high-poverty students becomes entirely academically focused to reduce academic inequities while at the same time increasing the unequal access to cultural capital, physical health, and joy in childhood. The youth development field can say with pride that some of the best after-school and summer programs are situated in urban contexts serving high-poverty students. ELTO can be effective in linking the school-day with these opportunities, expanding them, and making sure that all students have access to them. Access to better instruction for academic success has to go hand in hand with increased enrichment opportunities.

Quality use of time

Expanding school hours in itself does not guarantee increased student performance and can potentially minimize students' access to important positive youth development opportunities. To offer students diverse learning opportunities, some schools infuse community partners throughout a longer school day, altering enrichment and academic content. Others break up the day between the core academics and electives, and leave afternoons for nonformal activities. Edward Bleeker Junior High School, an expanded day community school in Queens, New York, for example, devotes equal time to academics, electives, and enrichment learning, along with on-site physical and mental health support services for students and their families. Creating engaging schedules that balance the academic core with civic and community projects, hands-on learning, twenty-first century skill building, or programs that promote socio–emotional development could potentially lead to positive student learning outcomes. For example, skills such as problem-solving, cooperation, communication, initiative and perseverance, teamwork, and flexible adaptation to innovation are becoming critically important in preparing students for future employment, and are the types of skills often adequately acquired through ELOs.

Relationship building

Effective ELTO partnerships have strong organizational capacities, joint professional development and decision-making systems, and a commitment to collaboration that improve and empower both partners and help students learn. ELT schools that partner with ELOs recognize that schools cannot do everything and that community partners can be an asset in supporting student learning and positive youth development. ELOs can bring a wealth of community and organizational resources to a school, providing students with learning and experiential opportunities they might not have had access to otherwise (e.g., the partnership between LA's BEST and Leo Politi Elementary School in Los Angeles). ELOs gain students (especially in mandatory agreements with schools) access to school facilities and resources. By partnering with quality ELOs, schools, in return, have the opportunity to offer teachers more flexibility to teach electives, devote additional time to common lesson planning, and access classroom aides provided by community partners (e.g., the partnership between Citizen Schools and Jane Long Middle School in Houston, Texas). Presence of ELOs on the school grounds can also attract families and lead to increased parental involvement. ELTO can help to provide a sense of community, rather than a feeling of more "institution," for a longer period of time. Productive relationships are essential to humanize the experience in the schools, both for youth and adults.

With more families working, parents' time with their children has decreased in both amount and intensity over the years. Enhancing mentoring opportunities in an ELTO context with sustained adult relationships in real-life settings can have positive effects on youth, reducing premature terminations of mentoring dyads that research has shown to be detrimental.

Commitment to data

Quality ELTO partners are committed to data; they share data, engage in evaluations to inform practice, and look to a broader set of indicators as guideposts for student learning and success. Although schools adhere to the No Child Left Behind guidelines to measure students' academic progress, many principals recognize the importance of assessing a variety of indicators—school attendance, classroom motivation and engagement, grades, and soft-skills acquisition. ELOs also track progress on multiple dimensions, often in congruence with their partner schools. LA's BEST engages in longitudinal third-party evaluations that inform the overall benefits of the individual organization's programs on student learning and development. TASC uses a two-pronged strategy, conducting independent evaluations and monitoring internal progress over time. Its Grad Tracker monitoring tool, for example, is designed to assess students' likelihood of on-time graduation, an early warning system that can help ELTO partnership tailor interventions to better support students.

Practical challenges

Creating effective ELTO partnerships poses several practical challenges—balancing school needs with those of a local community, designing staffing structures to support ELTO, selecting community partners, building safeguards for ELOs, and sustaining funding over time.

Local context or school goals?

While local context plays an important role, schools are afforded freedom to shape daily schedules and to customize students' learning experiences. The school-led expanded learning strategies bring up questions: How do schools balance mandates with local needs? Who decides what students' needs take priority and the delivery mechanism by which to meet them? Inviting community to the table and integrating their input could help build coherence and linkages between school and community needs.

The youth development philosophy that is fueling the community partners that often make up ELTO partnerships views young people as assets and active contributors. The idea is that youth, when allowed to show strength, empathy, and commitment, will engage in positive actions. Developing an ELTO partnership that links youth to civic projects, for example, can be a major benefit to students and community members alike and can also help bridge the divide between the generations. There are many good examples of youth visiting senior citizens' homes, volunteering with recycling projects, or developing oral histories in their communities.

Balancing the needs of families with school goals is another important consideration. The assurance working families receive that their child will be safe until five or six in the afternoon is paramount in decreasing chances of students spending their afternoons unsupervised in a potentially unsafe environment. Schools like Burroughs Elementary School in Chicago look to families for guidance on how to structure a longer learning day, what partners to bring on board, and how to more effectively engage families. Schools that see a boost in family involvement are those that create diverse entry points into schools, be that through PTAs, family resource centers on the school grounds, evening and weekend community education programs, and other pathways that offer families voice and presence within schools.

Who should staff expanded learning time?

Some schools in resource-poor communities turn to teachers to lead electives and additional extracurricular clubs, whereas others open such opportunities to community partners. The choice of who should staff the expanded schedule rests on multiple variables—principal leadership, school culture, teacher bargaining agreements, resources available to support programming in an extended schedule, access to quality community partners that could deliver a portion of expanded learning, and family, student, and community input.

To determine what staffing model might work best, many schools turn to site-based needs assessments to determine what interventions stand to benefit the students and what partners are best positioned to deliver them. Once the needs are determined, it is the combination of building a shared ELTO vision and goals, strong principal leadership that drives the ELTO culture, role differentiation between teachers and partners, presence of community liaisons, continuous access to technical assistance, professional development, collaboration, and joint planning that lead to a sustainable expanded day staffing model.

How are partners selected?

Although some schools open their doors to multiple partners and provide them flexibility to run their programs independently, other schools focus on targeted partnerships with providers that can help students meet specific academic goals. Although both parties must agree to the contours of their partnership, some ELO advocates see this relationship as potentially unbalanced. The fear is that some ELOs, to conform to the agreement with a school, might narrow their focus, specializing in only several key activities that could fit in a class period or a short morning or an afternoon session. This potentially unequal relationship between schools and partner organizations poses several core questions: Who has the authority to decide what role ELOs play in a given school? What are the safeguards for ELOs to operate within schools or in partnership with schools implementing expanded learning? Creating mutual agreements could help to address common issues of turf, use of school resources, and the role of ELO staff during the school day.

One of the common ways that ELT schools benefit from ELO partnerships during the school day is the availability of youth development professionals to contribute to the school day rather than staying confined to the afternoon hours. In ELTO partnerships, ELO staff from local YMCA's, Boys and Girls Clubs, or other youth serving organizations, actually participate in activities and lessons during the school day, such as lunch hours, field trips, or enrichment classes. One cannot underestimate the power these staff members have to help change school climate and to provide "near peer" engagement with students for learning.

What safeguards exist for ELOs?

The majority of the schools highlighted in this issue operate in resource-poor communities and serve high-poverty students. As a result, the relationships schools make with community partners are usually the only way some students get to access enrichment opportunities. By engaging external partners on the school grounds, children and youth have a familiar, safe, and structured space to attend from early morning until the evening at least five days a week. However, in areas where ELOs have a community presence, there are growing concerns about student choice and community organization opportunity, concerns that are yet to be adequately addressed in the field. For example, if a school integrates enrichment programs on the school grounds with targeted community partners, does that structure impede other ELOs not in partnership with a given school from gaining access to these same students? Given the long school hours, how can students pursue interests not offered in their school but available in the community? If schools are exclusively partnering with formal organizations and agencies, do students lose access to informal mentors and community volunteers that can also engage with them and offer both academic and enrichment support?

For students in low-resource areas, ELTO approach offers great benefits for planning, funding, and sustainability. For students whose out-of-school time options are to engage in sedentary TV or computer game activities, ELTO offers a choice for productive learning, academic support, and meaningful and enjoyable activities that students can partake in. This scenario was one of the important considerations for creating the out-of-school time movement and is the one driver within the ELTO strategy.

Is the expanded learning strategy financially sustainable?

Most ELTO partnerships gain funding through a blend of public and private funds. The federal government, for example, offers several funding streams that could be utilized by schools and community partners, such as Title I School Improvement Grants, Race to the Top, and Investing in Innovations (i3).

At the time of this issue production, several federal bills had been introduced in support of extending the school day and for expanded learning. The State and Local Funding Flexibility Act, H.R. 2445, introduced in the summer of 2011, for example, allows states and districts to shift 21st Century Community Learning Centers (CCLC) funds to and from after-school programs, in accordance with school needs. There is also discussion to open CCLC to expanded time and community schools. Additionally, a coalition of some forty organizations has also offered support in the summer of 2011 to The Time for Innovation Matters in Education (TIME) Act that would fund additional school hours.

With reauthorization of the Elementary and Secondary Education Act (ESEA) still pending and the national discourse focused on instruction, teachers, and test scores, uncertainties still remain: How will the new federal legislation support ELOs? What incentives will be in place to encourage ELTO partnerships? What safeguards will be in place to ensure that expanded time does not mean more core academic time?

In this austere fiscal climate, funding for innovative learning strategies is limited. As we go to press, there is a potential compromise on the table on the federal level to open funding streams for after-school programs, ELT schools, and ELTO strategies. However, it is important to recognize that there is no safeguard that funding directed toward ELT schools will be used to partner with ELOs. And, it is possible that new funding would privilege extended day practices over ELTO strategies. As long as this possibility looms, it is especially important that funding is evenly distributed among many approaches, including ELTO, and that there is continued support for free-standing after-school and summer programs; many who have existed for well over 100 years, have strong connections to their communities, and have grown organically. These programs are quite adapt to change and have shown remarkable willingness to join in helping kids achieve academically, something that even ten or twenty years ago was not a strong part of their missions. This issue is urgent, as it has divided the field and created unnecessary friction, even among those who share a common interest in innovative learning practices for students.

Conceptual challenges

As a nascent concept, ELTO faces several conceptual challenges—language ambiguity, lack of unified purpose, and inconsistent youth development programming integration.

Language ambiguity

As expanded learning strategy gains momentum on the education scene, language ambiguity persists. In this issue, the terms were defined based on models of practice that best emulate strong and successful school–community partnerships: ELOs—community-based organizations, agencies, and intermediaries who offer in-school, after-school, summer, or year-round programming services targeted to complement both academic and developmental goals; ELT schools—public schools that extend their schedules to include wider learning components and who utilize both the teaching staff and ELOs to create quality learning experiences for primarily high-poverty students; and ELTO—a partnership between ELT schools and ELOs.

However, the definitions applied in this issue are not uniformly used in the field. The notion of *expanded learning* can be associated with out-of-school-time programs or after-school programs, with schools that extend time devoted to the academic core subjects or schools that operate on a year-round basis, to full-service schools, or to innovations in experiential and digital learning. The ambiguity and inconsistency of the meaning of *expanded learning* transform the phrase into an umbrella term that encompasses a wide variety of school reform and developmental strategies. Although beneficial in bringing forth innovative ideas of how to support low-income youth, the vagueness of the term potentially leaves particular approaches vulnerable in policy debates.

The language issues, while seeming potentially trite, are actually very significant. The after-school and youth development fields, for example, have for decades struggled with self-definition on a linguistic level, which stands also as a problem in identity. After-school has never been a uniformly welcomed term because it defines itself as something that happens after something else, rather than being in itself an important and valuable practice. Out-of-school time, often meant to subsume after-school and summer programs, also defines itself as something that is not happening at school. However, with increasing programming at school and with integrated approaches between school, summer, and after-school, new terms are needed. ELTO as a term provides a new lens, focusing attention to a kind of educational practice, expanding schools to include outside partners. In order for ELTO as a term to be fully applicable, it has to demonstrate a strong educational focus and a strong commitment to connecting the youth development sphere to school learning. This, in fact, is happening at present.

Purpose

The current school reform debate gives ELOs an opportunity to supplement the school day by offering a range of programs that promote holistic development. Given the diversity of expanded learning implementation in schools, there is lack of clear purpose of what expanded learning as a strategy is ultimately designed to do. Is it to boost students' scores on standardized tests? Is it to help students graduate and continue on to college? Is it to help students meet developmental goals? As our authors note, a majority of schools with community partners see expanded learning as having a dual purpose—to help students achieve academically and to gain access to hands-on experiential learning in a safe, structured environment. However, in the public sphere, the nuances around both language and purpose remain largely unaddressed.

Youth development program integration

This issue specifically emphasizes the importance of expanding not only learning time but also opportunities for diverse learning. The presence of ELOs in schools reinforces the growing notion that schools need external support to meet increasing demands placed on them by governmental policies and the society. Many ELOs serve to support both the academic goals set forth by the partner schools and student-centered developmental goals. For instance, community schools with expanded learning strategies are particularly well positioned to cultivate broader youth development goals because of coordinated efforts with a range of community providers and service agencies. However, as school reform remains the main driver of expanded learning policies, there is risk that broader youth development goals might take a back seat to core academic goals.

Next steps

The old, traditional school schedule is not working. As both President Obama and educators in the field alike warn, for the United States to stay competitive on a global level, we need to rethink our education system, paying attention, among other areas, to time—how much time students spend in formal, nonformal, and informal learning spaces. Short school days that no longer accommodate working families or meet academic goals, and unstructured summers that often leave disadvantaged students with summer learning loss, are inadequate to help students get through our primary and secondary education system or complete postsecondary degrees. The dropout crisis facing many urban schools further illustrates this problem and pushes reformers to reexamine our schools' use of time in both length and substance.

However, time alone, particularly more of the same, is unlikely to help students succeed. Expanding time and learning opportunities are important elements to positive youth development. There are three key steps that proponents of expanded learning, in its broadest sense, could take to improve practice, invest in research, and gain sustainability through targeted policies—invest in a broader vision of expanded learning, focus on comprehensive evidence-based strategies, and create a unified advocacy message to sustain and grow funding streams that support quality learning experiences for children and youth.

Invest in a broader vision of expanded learning

There is a growing chorus of voices within education circles that acknowledge the need to address a wider set of student needs through schools and in partnership with community organizations.[3] Investing in an expanded learning strategy that has a whole-child focus stands to help disadvantaged students gain well-rounded educational experiences that can help them successfully progress through the K–12 system and beyond. When serving students in resource-poor communities, schools are often an effective delivery mechanism for diverse learning opportunities, and community intermediaries are established brokers for a wide set of children and youth services. Maximizing the expertise of each of the stakeholders allows both schools and community partners to focus on their area of expertise and collaborate in a way that offers students a broad range of learning experiences throughout the day and year, both formal and nonformal, cognitive and noncognitive.

This broader vision also helps to incorporate socio-emotional health, which promotes productive learning, a third leg of a stool on which we all, and children and youth, stand. There is no productive learning in an expanded day without socio-emotional well-being. When children are worried about being bullied or when they are depressed, learning will recede into the background. Mentoring and nonformal learning environments offer space where caring ELTO adults can help bring out many issues that have a socio-emotional and mental health valiance. Children typically like to tell their stories when they feel that adults are listening. ELTO provides the opportunity to access student support services during the school day that are usually not available to freestanding after-school programs or those that are in school buildings, but not integrated. Such services, if situated and linked to schools—for psychologists, nurses, social workers—are an important protective step for the kids served.

Focus on comprehensive evidence-based strategies

Data-driven accountability is becoming standard practice both in schools and among ELOs. Educators and youth development professionals are increasingly required by their funders to provide evidence of effectiveness on diverse sets of measures. For schools, the yardstick is standardized state test scores; for community partners, it is a group of funder-driven indicators, from student participation levels and demographic information to relationships between program outcomes and in-school student success. Emerging data show that ELT schools can be successful in boosting student learning by implementing a variety of strategies, including partnering with ELOs. There is also a growing body of research noted in this issue's chapters that shows positive relationships between quality ELO experiences and students' in-school performance.

However, because of the high level of ELTO partnership variability, there is a lack of comprehensive evidence linking any one particular expanded learning approach with a particular set of results. Investing in longitudinal evaluations, controlled experiments, and data sharing across ELTO partners could help to build a more robust case for expanded learning. Further, although test scores are a common measure of school reform success or failure, if the goal is to get students ready for college and career, a single gauge is not enough. Finally, the emerging data-driven culture requires investments in staff training on how to collect and use data, how to conduct internal evaluations and assessments, and how to integrate data to improve practice. It is only with consistent, quality data and use of that data that we can improve, grow, and make a stronger case for expanded learning.

Create a unified advocacy message

Federal and state governments, along with philanthropic organizations and the business sector, provide backing for expanded learning strategies and offer diverse funding streams to support such efforts. However, a lack of clear language, purpose, and goals that could drive a unified message of what expanded learning is and could be at times is polarizing the debate between school supporters and youth development advocates. As the FrameWorks Institute noted in a previous issue of this journal (#124), the public is often unaware of the benefits of particular educational and developmental strategies, the differences and similarities among strategies, or the need for continuous or greater investment in such strategies. A unified message that joins advocacy efforts in education and child- and youth development sectors stands both to preserve the existing funding streams and to encourage creation of broader, more flexible funding opportunities that could help both schools and community-based organizations.

A unified ELTO message is particularly important in empowering community-based organizations that offer ELOs to have an equal voice in funding allocation debates. Unlike schools, the youth development field is not politically organized. There is no federal agency for youth development advocates like the U.S. Department of Education. There is no consistent, robust, state-level coordination engine. And, although some intermediaries play an important role on the local levels, they do not compare in budget and power to the school districts. This leads to a complicated situation for youth organizations, even those who have joined schools to reach their goals. This is also the reason why special safeguards need to be put in place by policy makers and by the coalitions making up ELTO. Joint decision-making, multi-year funding, and a joint definition of outcomes are key to sustaining strong ELTO partnerships.

Conclusion

Expanded learning is focused on helping students succeed; it is available to most, if not all, students in a given school; it creates learning continuity; and it demands stakeholder commitment. ELTO partnerships offer disadvantaged students equitable access to quality education, enrichment, and development opportunities and help them overcome adversity.

As illustrated in this issue's chapters, a growing number of schools are considering ways to expand the learning day as a way to break the mold from traditional school schedules. Schools and community organizations that engage in expanded learning together believe that students need quality instruction and active learning that reinforces school curriculum and also offers students opportunities to explore their own interests and passions. Theoretical arguments and promising practices illustrated in this issue illuminate one aspect of expanded learning, the important role ELOs play in ELT schools and the promise ELTO partnerships hold in creating meaningful learning experiences for students in high-poverty communities.

Notes

1. Investments range from government-funded opportunities—Race to the Top, Investment in Innovation, School Improvement Grants—to philanthropic investments such as the Gates and Eli Broad Foundations.

2. Learning Point Associates and The Collaborative for Building After-School Systems. (2010). *Integrating expanded learning and school reform initiatives: Challenges and strategies.* Naperville, IL: Authors; McLaughlin, B., & Phillips, T. L. (2009). *Meaningful linkages between summer programs, schools, and community partners: Conditions and strategies for success.* Baltimore, MD: National Summer Learning Association; Traphagen, K., & Johnson-Staub, C. (2010). *Expanded time, enriching experiences: Expanded learning time schools and community organization partnerships.* Washington, DC: Center for American Progress.

3. Blank, M., & Berg, A. (2006, July). *All together now: Sharing responsibility for the whole child.* Alexandria, VA: Association for Supervision and Curriculum Development; Fiske, T., & Rosenberg, B. (2007). *A broader, bolder approach to education.* Retrieved from http://www.boldapproach.org; Grossman, J. B., & Vang, Z. M. (2009). *The case for school-based integration of services: Changing the ways students, families, and communities engage with their schools.* Philadelphia, PA: Public/Private Ventures; Harvard Family Research Project. (2010, March). *Partnerships for learning: Promising practices in integrating school and out-of-school time program supports.* Cambridge, MA: Author.

HELEN JANC MALONE *is an advanced doctoral candidate at the Harvard Graduate School of Education focusing on youth development and education policy research.*

GIL G. NOAM *is editor-in-chief of the New* Directions for Youth Development *journal, the founder and director of the Program in Education, Afterschool & Resiliency (PEAR), and an associate professor at Harvard Medical School and McLean Hospital.*

Index